The KITCHEN HANDBOOK

BY SALLY KING

PELHAM BOOKS

First published in Great Britain by
Pelham Books Ltd
27 Wright's Lane
Kensington
London W8
1986

Designed and produced by
Johnson Editions Ltd
15 Grafton Square
London SW4 0DQ

British Library Cataloguing in Publication Data
King, Sally
        The kitchen handbook.
        1. Kitchens-Remodelling-Amateurs' manuals
        I. Title
        643'.3 TX653

ISBN 0-7207-1657-8

Editor: Gabrielle Townsend
Designer: Lorraine Johnson
Production: Landmark Production Consultants
Typesetting: Fowler Printing Services
Origination: ScanTrans, Singapore
Printed and bound in Hong Kong by
Mandarin Offset Marketing (H.K.) Ltd.

CONTENTS

The Dream Kitchen is dead. That is, the Dream that assumed the same kitchen was the ideal for everyone and everyone had the same dream.

What is true today is that designing your own kitchen is a highly individual matter — it must suit you, your family, your way of cooking, eating and living.

The aim of this Handbook is to help you achieve your own "dream" kitchen.

One of the problems everyone faces when planning a kitchen today is the huge choice. Hundreds of appliances. Thousands of units. Kitchen planners galore. And they are all waiting, if not jostling, to be part of your kitchen. How do you sort them out? How do you find just what you want — in your price range?

This Handbook has been designed to help you find your way through this maze, and to give you an idea of the principles behind the choices facing you. On the following pages you'll see some of the best new ideas from the top manufacturers and designers alongside ingenious ways of making-do.

You'll also see that the first step towards your "dream" kitchen is, in a way, a voyage of discovery about yourself. Until you have thought quite deeply about the way you want to live you can't translate what you need into a basic plan for a kitchen, let alone a colour scheme, a cooker or a set of kitchen units.

Begin by asking yourself a lot of questions: how you like to cook, who you cook for, who else cooks, how you like to entertain, whether you have to cater for small children or not, whether you feel you are basically a formal person or an informal one?

After a little analysis, you can start building up your own ideas as you read this handbook. It is divided into seven different, but interacting, sections:

A historical perspective. How kitchens have always reflected the life (and prosperity) of their owners.

Choosing your style. How the style of a kitchen relates both to its function and situation in the house.

Planning your kitchen. How to work out what you need and make your own plan.

Choosing the storage. Do you need units? If so — which? If not — some alternatives.

Choosing the hardware. How to evaluate function and style in sinks, dishwashers, cookers, pots and pans, fridges, freezers, larders and store cupboards.

Decorating schemes. How to design your own, and choose practical wall, floor and ceiling coverings and lighting to complement it.

Plus and minus. How to get eating into the kitchen, and laundry, etc, out of it.

Below. A sink unit that combines tradition with hi-tech. Designer Michael Reed has strengthened and trimmed 5cm/2in-thick solid beech with Colorcore (TM) — the new colour-all-through plastic laminate material.

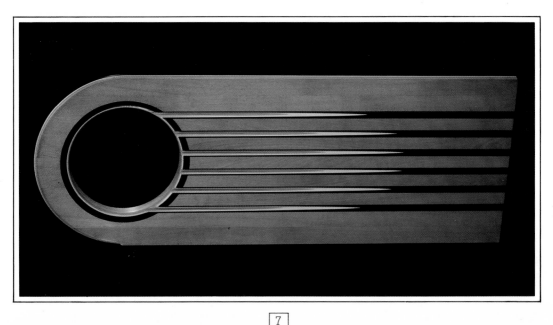

Planning a new kitchen or re-thinking an old one is a major undertaking today. But it wasn't always so. In the past, hundreds of years went by before anyone launched a new cooker or thought up a new style for cupboards.

Kitchens reflect their owners' needs and aspirations accurately. Progress is only made when an incentive arises to improve the kitchen, and when enough money is available to spend on it. The slow evolution of the British kitchen, as shown below, demonstrates this.

British working class kitchens — whether in industrial towns or country cottages — had remained very basic for hundreds of years. No one could afford improvements.

In America, on the other hand, the story was very different. There the newly-prosperous middle classes experienced the Servantless Kitchen as early as the 1860s, whereas in Britain servants were plentiful until the 1920s. Early feminists, like Catherine Beecher, urged American women not to put up with unnecessary housework and to insist on labour-saving kitchens — she admired ship's galleys particularly for their streamlined efficiency — and felt the time and energy saved ought to give women more time to do interesting things.

This meant that, over the years, American manufacturers had the incentive to introduce and market the first gas and electric cookers to the general public, and to pioneer and develop

Below. The Traditional Family Kitchen

Here the whole family lived, cooking, eating, sleeping and working together in the same room. Less than 100 years ago people in the Orkneys lived in kitchens such as this. Simply moving the fire from the centre of the room to a side wall so that smoke went up a chimney instead of through a hole in the roof was the first breakthrough in kitchen planning! The second was the arrival of the closed range for cooking. Benjamin Franklin patented his Philadelphia stove in the 1740s but most people had to wait for one until after the Industrial Revolution, by which time cast iron could be mass-produced and coal for the stoves could be transported cheaply and easily by rail.

Below. The Labour-Intensive Kitchen

This is typical of the kitchens found in the houses of wealthy Victorians. These kitchens were efficient establishments designed to cater for the needs of large families, many guests and numerous servants. They were well-planned, with plenty of space and good quality equipment. A big kitchen table was the main work surface, cooking was done on a huge range, and big dressers in the kitchen itself plus various sculleries, pantries, larders and even ice-houses provided storage space. As there were plenty of servants to scrub and scour, peel and scrape, fetch and carry, those who could have afforded to improve their kitchens had no incentive to do so.

all sorts of labour-saving devices. Automatic washing machines, vacuum cleaners, dish-washers, refrigerators, freezers, food processors were all commonplace in American kitchens long before anyone considered them necessary in Britain. And one of the first people to take kitchen design seriously was the American architect Frank Lloyd Wright. In 1940 he designed a private house where "for the first time the space of the kitchen (called the work space) is joined to that of the living room". He gave the kitchen continuous work surfaces, fitted storage space and all available modern conveniences.

Since the Sixties, the major changes in kitchen design are the result of new technologies and the increasingly informal way we now live.

Technology has given us electronically-controlled appliances, greatly improved laminates, better-designed units and much more effective ventilation. As more women have jobs outside the home, it has become doubly important for the kitchen to be as convenient and labour-saving as possible.

As we adapt the kitchen to the way we live today, three sorts of kitchens emerge. **The Unkitcheny Kitchen** – part of the main living area and designed so it does not obtrude visually. **The Family Kitchen** – furnished as a kitchen but used as the focal point for much of the life of the household. **The Kitchen Workshop** – designed to be the most efficient food production unit for the particular household using it.

Below. The Compact Kitchen

Linked to the dining room or main living-room by a hatch, this became the ideal in Britain during the 1920s and 1930s, when the Servantless House became a reality, and Victorian kitchens were impractical, if not impossible, to run single-handed. Although most women at this time still perceived their place as being in the home, they wished to keep their roles as cook and kitchen maid separate from their other activities. Many people still prefer this arrangement and it is the norm in much post-war housing. Its main disadvantage is that there is often no room for new or bigger labour-saving equipment nor for informal meals.

Below. The Family Kitchen

New thinking about kitchens emerged in the 1960s — spurred on by women's lib, more informal patterns of family life and entertainment, new interest in good cooking and, above all, relative prosperity. People like the architect John Prizeman showed how basements of terrace houses could be brought to life as spacious all-purpose family kitchens with fitted storage, split-level cookers, large built-in appliances, continuous work surfaces and ergonomically correct planning. New materials and finishes made everything easier to clean and maintain. There was also space for family meals, small children to play safely, the pursuit of hobbies and often a sofa for relaxing or watching TV.

Unkitcheny Kitchens first appeared in open-plan houses and flats after the Second World War. Now they are the ideal solution when houses are opened up by knocking down walls between smaller rooms so that the kitchen becomes merely one area within a larger living space. It is not totally shut off or hidden (although its limits are probably defined in some way) so the kitchen area has to harmonise with the rest of the room.

It is a civilised way to live. No one has to disappear to produce meals, snacks, drinks or cups of coffee and when you entertain, you are never far from your guests, even while you work.

Special Features of The Unkitcheny Kitchen

• Decor and units which do not shriek 'Kitchen!' are essential. Unless the cooking area is concealed round a corner, its elements must be sympathetic to the rest of the room. For instance, matching the wood of the units to that of the dining table, bookcases, coffee table and so on. Similarly, in a High Tech conversion, you would continue that style.

• Conceal all appliances behind integrated doors so that the run of cupboards isn't interrupted visually.

• If a different floor covering is chosen to demarcate the kitchen area, its colours and textures should match or complement that in the main living area.

• Other decorative elements such as the tiles, wallpaper, pictures, etc, must also follow the style of the living room. Avoid all those kitcheny clichés like gingham checks, strings of onions, butchers' chopping blocks, kitchen Victoriana.

• Extremely good ventilation is essential if you do not want cooking smells to dominate your life — see pages 32-33.

• Keep the working part of the kitchen as compact as possible, arranged in an L-shape or straight line — see pages 16-17.

• If there's only enough space for a tiny compact kitchen in the living space, consider shutting it off behind cupboard doors — see pages 38-39.

• Green plants and uncluttered work tops all contribute to the living room atmosphere of the Unkitcheny Kitchen.

Opposite: Two views of a living room and kitchen which share an effective pared-down style for table and units.

Above: Handsome dark wood units match chairs to create quite a formal "dining room" look.

Below: Natural wood units here make compatible partners to cane easy chairs and coffee table.

Family kitchens, though designed primarily for cooking and eating, provide for lots of other activities as well. The aim is to create the busy, friendly atmosphere of an old-fashioned country kitchen. Nostalgia in the States harks back to the Mexican ranch or the early pioneer kitchens, in Europe to traditional Breton, Norman and Alsatian styles.

A good family kitchen is spacious enough for family meals, for small children to play safely, for older ones to do homework or hobbies and for adults to relax comfortably between chores. It is the centre of informal family life.

Features that good Family Kitchens have in common

• Developments since the Sixties have been dominated by nostalgia, hence the enormous revival in the popularity of wood, particularly pine, whether old or new, stripped or painted. (Old pine furniture can be successfully converted into units — see pages 36–37). Dark, carved oak is favoured in America and in Europe, although the Scandinavians still prefer paler woods such as birch or ash.

• Other natural materials are preferred — for floors, quarry tiles, wood, cork, stone or slate are in keeping. But today they're treated with practical, wipe-clean finishes.

• Include things that look handmade: wooden doors that are dragged, grained or stencilled; irregular hand-made tiles; a few antiques such as old cooking implements, vintage packaging, flowery china.

• Large, functional appliances, not necessarily built-in, enhance the comfortable, practical mood, for instance a wood or solid fuel stove for cooking, water heating, or just to sit by.

• Ideally banish laundry to a utility room.

• Big wooden table for sitting around, working on, eating at.

• Room for young children — perhaps storage bins for toys, space for a playpen, and a special low table.

• If there are teenagers you'll need facilities for endless snacks, a large fridge/freezer, sandwich toaster, perhaps a microwave. Plus the essential dishwasher.

• Somewhere to relax: a comfortable sofa for watching TV. Radio and telephone so you don't feel cut off if you spend long periods in the kitchen.

• A homely atmosphere — family kitchens are not over-tidy, sophisticated places. They spill over with children's pictures, seeds sprouting, baskets of knitting and havens for pets.

Right: The same kitchen with the family in action in it! There's plenty of room for a school project to be organised on the kitchen table, while quick snacks, and cat talk, go on at the breakfast bar.

Above and opposite: Comfort and informality are the keynotes of this family kitchen which embraces a sitting room, somewhere to eat as well as a well-equipped work area. Wood is used throughout — on the floor and for the pale green dragged units.

The trend today is to treat self-contained kitchens used only for food preparation as workshops, and make them as streamlined and efficient as possible. The term "Workshop" implies practicality and fitness for purpose and, in a Kitchen Workshop, everything is adapted and arranged to suit the individual household's need.

Some Workshop Kitchens will be elaborate. They might be specially designed for professional or deeply committed cooks and could include several fridges, a set of sharp knives kept in special blocks and exceptionally good quality sets of pans and utensils, hanging, where they are needed, over the cooker. Others will be workshops dedicated to the daily chore of feeding a family, to baking for the WI or the local football team, to producing quantities of jam or marmalade in season, to freezing the produce

Below: A professional's workshop — a chef's kitchen designed by architect Theo Crosby. Note the compact work area, the closed storage, the easily-reached utensils over the cooker, the sinks which can be used from either side, the practical all-in-one stainless steel sink and worktop. And the simple, but visually effective, use of tiling.
See page 55 for a close-up view of the worktop.

of a prolific garden and to creating elaborate dinners. Yet others might be minimal — designed to produce occasional snacks with the greatest possible speed and efficiency.

All these workshops have one criterion in common — to be as functional as possible.

What makes a good Kitchen Workshop?

• Careful planning. It is vital to work out exactly what you want to cook in your workshop. The work-surfaces, the appliances, the cooker, the work — how can they be organised as efficiently as possible?

• Storage also needs careful planning. Different kinds of cooking have different storage needs. New ways to use storage space more effectively are being introduced all the time and are valuable space savers in small workshops — (see pages 52-53).

• Ease of cleaning and maintenance is important. Workshops can look pretty, but are not efficient unless finishes, surfaces, etc, are hard-wearing and easy to keep clean.

• Good ventilation can cut out a lot of day-to-day cleaning because the greasy fumes do not remain in the kitchen to settle on shelves, surfaces, etc.

- Good quality implements and appliances increase efficiency whatever is being prepared.

- Effective lighting — both daylight and at night — creates the right working environment. (See pages 88-91).

- Although decor is secondary to efficiency in a Kitchen Workshop, there is opportunity to be imaginative. While still preserving an uncluttered, streamlined look, you can achieve a dramatic effect through the use of colour — brilliant white or bold primaries.

- If you have to choose a Workshop because space is limited, try and fit in a table top for snacks. Some units have a pull-out table which could usefully double as an extra work surface. Chairs can be folded and hung on the back of the kitchen door or a cupboard when not in use.

Above: A workshop kitchen which could be the prototype of how to maximise limited space at one end of a large living room as a kitchen. It is an open U-shape plan with a continuous run of worktop and units; a large built-in fridge-freezer is tucked away on the right, its side attractively disguised with shelves of plants. The hob and oven are set at an angle in the corner to provide a comfortable position for cooking. Lighting and extractor fan are concealed behind a wooden panel above. The units provide all necessary storage and have practical glossy white laminate doors with natural wood surrounds and handles. Their proportions are good so that the pattern made by the doors, drawers and oven is pleasingly balanced, but not too obtrusive. The table is strategically placed to cut off the kitchen area from the rest of the room — but it could be moved up to provide a temporary extra work surface for ambitious cooking sessions.

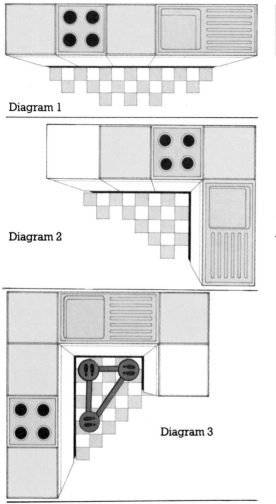

Diagram 1

Diagram 2

Diagram 3

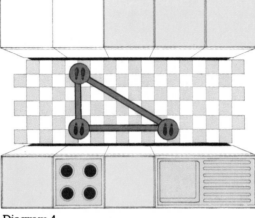

Diagram 4

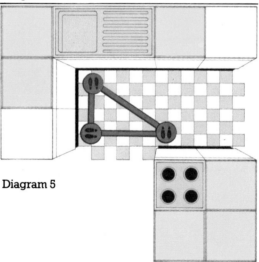

Diagram 5

The theory

The purpose of careful planning is to make it possible for you to do the work as easily and efficiently as possible.

Probably no two people would come up with exactly the same ideal kitchen, but there has been enough research done on how we tackle tasks like preparing food, cooking it and clearing it away, for a few basic rules to have emerged.

The work sequence

When thinking of all the different jobs involved in preparing and clearing away the simplest meal, you realise that most of them take place around three centres of activity: where the food is stored (in the refrigerator, freezer, larder or store cupboard), where some of the preparation and most of the clearing up is done (the sink), and the cooker. The secret of good kitchen planning lies in the way these centres are linked. Efficiency studies have shown that the work sequence is

most convenient if it follows this pattern: food storage — work surface — sink — work surface — cooker — work surface.

The simplest plan is to have a continuous work surface linking all these areas — see diagram 1. Surprisingly, everything can be fitted into a run of only 300cm/10ft, but becomes unwieldy when it is longer than 480cm/16ft. The continuous work sequence need not be in a straight line, however. It works equally well in an L-shape (see Diagram 2) or a U-shape (see Diagram 3).

The work triangle

This is another way of looking at the work sequence. It is especially valuable for kitchens where the work sequence has to be broken or if a great deal of space is available. Research into ergonomics (the study of the relationship between workers and their environment) at Cornell University in the early 1950s showed that there were crucial or maximal distances between these three centres — the food store, the sink and the cooker. These form the Work Triangle and in an efficient kitchen the three sides together should add up to no more than 6.6m/21ft 6in but no less than 3.6m/11ft 10in.

Diagrams 3, 4 and 5 demonstrate (with Work Triangles marked) some ways to plan a U-shaped kitchen, a galley kitchen and a kitchen with an island unit.

Some dimensions to consider

1. Worktop height
This nearly always has to be a compromise. The most comfortable height for the work surface is 15cm/6in below the level of your elbows. But as heights (and elbow measurements) vary, even among members of the same family, ideal worktop heights will also vary. To complicate matters, different countries consider different heights as "normal". In the UK 91cm/36in is standard, though taller people must feel the need for something higher. In Germany the assumption is that 86.5cm/34½in is normal, but some adjustment is allowed by varying the plinth height.

2. Worktop depth
Standard depth, from front to back, of a worktop is 600mm/24in and fortunately units, cookers and other appliances are being standardised to fit into or under this. Deeper worktops are no disadvantage — you simply have more worktop space, maybe to fit in some of the new Midway units or housings for appliances like food processors. It doesn't matter if the backs of the unit underneath won't reach right back to the wall. However, narrower worktops do create problems, because standard units and appliances will not fit under them.

3. Widths and heights of appliances
Standardisation, mentioned above, greatly simplifies kitchen planning. Many appliances today are made to standard dimensions — 600mm × 600mm × 850mm /24in × 24in × 34in high — to fit under worktops or into tall housing units. Units themselves are also usually standard heights and depths (normally on the 600mm module) but the better manufacturers offer an additional choice of widths, some as many as 12, ranging from 200mm to 1200mm. This should enable you to fit the most awkwardly shaped kitchen!

4. Comfortable cupboards
Other dimensions to consider are to do with bending down and reaching up. This affects how you plan your storage. Diagram 6 shows how to gauge your reach for the tops and bottoms of shelves and cupboards. Even if you have a good set of steps, it is not practical to have cupboards above 250cm/8ft. If the ceiling is over 8ft, the space between it and the top of any cupboards can be used for storing infrequently used (but

preferably light) objects or for displaying decorative features such as posters, dried flowers, etc.

5. Table heights
The optimal table to work or eat at is 71cm/2ft 4in high. If you want to use a worktop (normally 91cm/36in in height) as a bar for snack meals, you will need high stools.

Diagram 6 shows acceptable averages for worktop and cupboard heights — ideal for anyone 5ft 4in tall. It's easy enough to work out your own ideal, but some compromise is necessary if others are to use the kitchen too.

Max. cupboard height
250cm/8ft

Max. shelf height
180cm/
5ft 11in

Worktop height
91cm/36in

Worktop depth
60cm/24in

Table height
71cm/28in

Diagram 6

The Well-Planned Work Triangle

1. Work flows in a logical sequence

2. Work triangle (between sink, cooker and fridge) is ideally 4.5m/15ft.

3. Worktop is 91cm/36in high and provides a work surface each side of the sink and the cooker, and may include a chopping board near one or the other.

4. Fridge freezer has fridge above and freezer below to minimise bending down.

5. Hob is big enough to take large pans.

6. Heatproof panel on worktop beside cooker for resting hot pans.

7. Storage for pans near cooker.

8. Storage and drainage for china, glasses, cutlery near sink.

9. No doors or passageways interrupting the triangle.

10. Specific lighting over cooker (often concealed in extractor fans), sink and worktop.

11. Double sink with waste disposal unit in second sink.

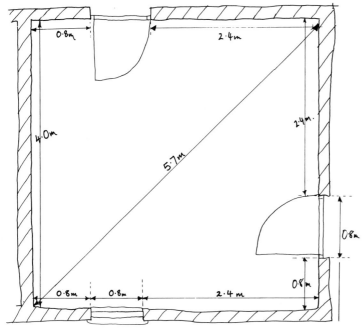

Diagram 1

Diagram 2

Step 1: Define the kind of kitchen you want.

Decide what style you like. One of the ways professional decorators do this is to advise the client to cut out pictures from magazines and brochures, of everything which appeals. The decorator can then take an overview, selecting those which are practicable in the kitchen. Some considerations are: how will the kitchen fit into your house or flat? Do you prefer wood finishes, monochromatic high tech, bright primary colours, or old-fashioned blue and white? What kind of kitchen suits your sort of cooking, entertaining and family life? Do you want to eat in the kitchen — always, sometimes, never? Do you have to allow for children, teenagers or older people? Check your ideas against other kitchens you have experienced. All this will help you define your own ideas and make decisions.

Step 2: List everything you want to do and keep in the kitchen

In addition to normal cooking and clearing away, include activities such as eating, snacking, laundry, ironing, children playing, sewing, paperwork, telephoning, watching TV, feeding pets, etc. Then list the appliances you have and any you want to acquire in the near future (so you can allow space for them). Note everything else you want to keep in the kitchen — from pots and pans to plants and photographs. You will then have a realistic idea of your own needs.

Step 3: Measure up and draw your plan

Make an accurate floor plan first. See left for a sample plan. Cut out shapes of appliances, units, tables, chairs, etc., to scale to work out how they will all fit in. At this stage you sometimes see an easy and obvious way to enlarge or open up the kitchen or to make the kind of minor structural improvements discussed on pages 26-27.

Step 4: Check the practicality of your plan

If the kitchen is empty, it will be easy to test out a work triangle on your plan. Pace out the triangle, allowing for units and appliances, on the floor and chalk dimensions on the walls. If and when you get to the stage of choosing units from a retailer, use his planning service (which is free) to check your ideas against.

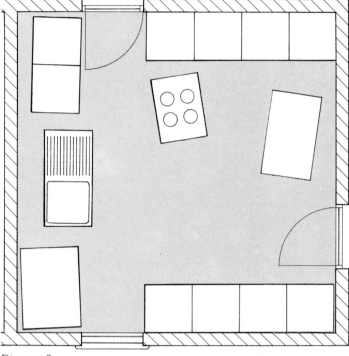

How to make your own scale plan

Diagram 3

1. Make a rough floor plan of the room. Measure dimensions of all inner walls and openings such as doors and windows and mark locations of plumbing, gas and electric points. Write down the measurements on your rough plan (diagram 1).

Diagram 4

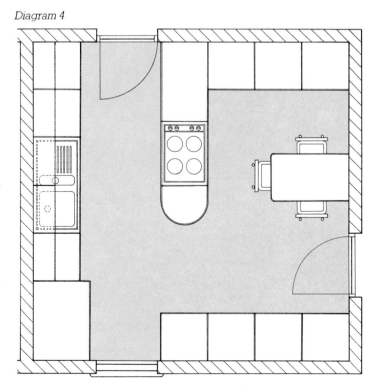

2. Next draw a scale plan. Either use squared paper and decide how many inches or centimetres each square will represent. Or use plain paper and the professional's scale of 1:20 — i.e. each centimetre on the paper representing 20 centimetres in the room (diagram 2).
3. Measure width and depth of appliances, sinks, units, tables, chairs, etc and cut out these shapes, using the same scale as above. Shuffle these around on the masterplan made in Step 2 to find the best arrangement (diagram 3).
4. Use tracing paper to make extra copies of the masterplan quickly and consider alternatives easily. (This is cheaper in the end than getting and paying for photocopies.)
5. Your final scale plan of the floor and the walls might turn out like diagram 4.

More accidents happen in the kitchen than any other room in the home. You can prevent some by planning your kitchen with these commonsense rules in mind:

• Even, non-slip floor surface that is easy to clean.

• Storage within easy reach. Stable steps or stool for high cupboards and shelves.

• Generous, uncluttered continuous work surface.

• Electrical appliances BEAB-approved and regularly serviced.

• Sufficient electric sockets so there are no trailing flexes, overloaded adaptors.

• Gas appliances with Gas Council's Seal of Approval and/or BSI Standard.

• Good task lighting over sink, worktop and cooker, and good general lighting everywhere.

• Hygienic food handling and storage (see pages 72-77).

More fires start in the kitchen than any other room. And many of these start because a chip-pan is allowed to overheat. These are some sensible precautions:

• Make it a rule never to have a chip pan heating unattended.

• Keep a fire blanket near the hob. If a fat fire does break out, throwing the blanket over the pan is the most effective way to smother the fire.

• Have a heat-resistant surface built in, or kept, beside hob and oven for hot pans and casseroles to stand on. Tiles or stainless steel are best.

• Avoid keeping anything (i.e. curtains, tea towels airing, aerosol cans, paper, paraffin) that could catch fire easily near the hob, or any heat source.

• Keep chimneys regularly swept.

Planning to protect the under-fives

When there are young children and babies around, kitchens need to be planned so both food and drink can be prepared in properly hygienic conditions and to protect young children from the results of their natural curiosity. Dangerous things must be kept out of their reach and the following guidelines observed:

• Floors must be easy to maintain but non-slippery (see pages 78-83).

• Easy-to-clean, continuous worktop for maximum hygiene in food preparation.

• Arrange storage with only harmless and unbreakable things within a small child's reach; if china and glass have to be kept in low cupboards, fit child-proof catches — even rubber bands round pairs of handles will do temporarily!

• Detergents, first aid supplies, indeed anything that could be poisonous if eaten, should be out of reach, again if possible behind child-proof locks.

• Concealed gas taps fitted with safety devices.

• Adult-level electric sockets or low-level ones fitted with dummy plugs.

• Guard around cooker so child cannot pull pan off.

• Small electrical appliances stored above child level.

• No tablecloths!

• Play area and toy storage away from main work triangle. Use playpen for toddlers if possible.

• Pet food, baskets and litter kept elsewhere.

Planning to make life easier for the over-seventies

Old people often have to soldier on in out-of-date kitchens, but they, more than anyone else, need the most up-to-date, labour-saving appliances and ideas, the most easy-to-maintain floors and worktops. These are points to consider when planning for over-seventies:

• Non-slip, level floor.

• Storage arranged so there is less bending down and climbing up to reach things. Wall ovens, for example, are easier to manage than ordinary cookers.

• Safety switches on gas appliances.

• If an electric kettle is used, make sure it has an automatic cut-off.

• Long-handled taps are easier for arthritic hands to manage.

• Touch latches or magnetic catches on cupboards.

• Drawers with stops so they can't be accidentally pulled out.

• Communication to outside world by intercom or telephone and entryphone for security, if appropriate.

• Dishwasher — even a small one — saves one tiring chore.

Opposite: Some do's and don'ts — clockwise from left:
DO have firm steps if you need to reach high cupboards or shelves.
DO keep detergents, bleaches, cleaners, medicines well out of children's reach.
DO have a fire blanket near the cooker to smother fat fires quickly.
DO choose lever taps for anyone whose hands are not strong.
DON'T economise on electric sockets so you have to use adaptors and overload the circuit.

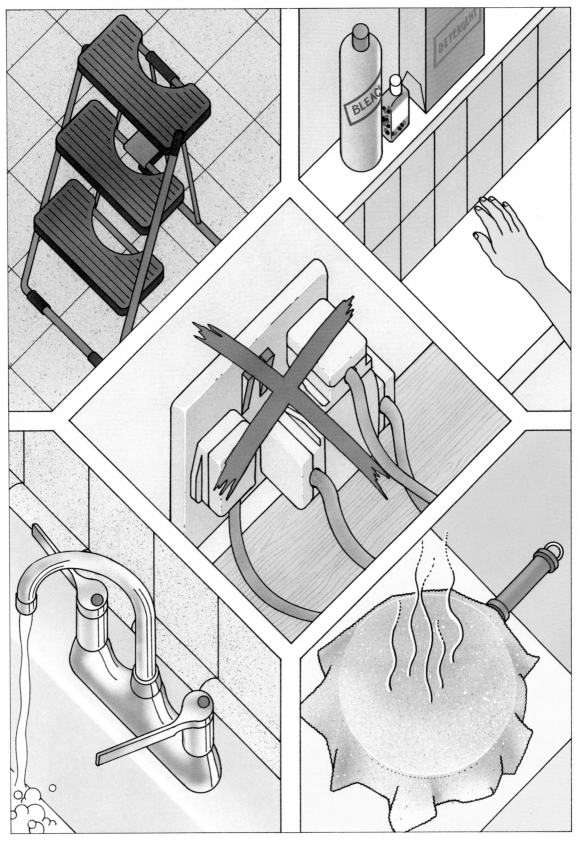

Very similar basic plans can vary tremendously in what they cost — depending on the units and appliances you choose, and the amount of structural work needed. Before you can make a realistic plan you must decide on a Budget. Is it to be £10s, £100s or £1,000s?

Raising the money

A new kitchen often turns out to be a very good investment. It not only adds significantly to the value of your home, but, when you come to sell, a good kitchen can make all the difference between a quick sale and one that hangs fire. It is also a pleasanter place for you meanwhile. So you may well feel justified in borrowing money to pay for bringing your kitchen up to date.

What a Home Improvement Loan can cover

For much of the work you can take out a Home Improvement loan on the same tax-efficient basis as your mortgage, with a similar simplified system of repayment. This means that, in effect, income tax is deducted at source at the standard rate from any interest paid on the loan. The system is known as MIRAS and supersedes the former arrangement whereby permitted loan interest was refunded via your tax coding. Your eligibility for tax relief is the same as that for your mortgage — i.e. the total amount (loan and mortgage) must not come to more than £30,000.

Work which qualifies for a Home Improvement Loan includes among other things: kitchen units, installation of water heating, some forms of central heating, rewiring, roof or wall insulation, double glazing, replacing windows and doors and — good to know about if you want to build on — home extensions. In other words, it covers much of the work needed to renovate a kitchen. But this particular type of loan is not normally available for work on second homes.

Home Improvement Loans on these terms can be taken out through a Bank, a Building Society, a Finance House or an Insurance Company with whom you have a life or endowment policy. You can arrange a Home Improvement Loan yourself or, you'll find, most kitchen suppliers have a tie-up and will make the arrangements for you. Home Improvement Loans cannot cover new appliances. But you can finance these as Credit Sales in the normal way — many retailers will give you free credit for limited periods.

Are you entitled to a Home Improvement Grant?

If you are, this is free money! Home Improvement Grants are administered by local councils and are intended to help bring sub-standard homes below a certain rateable value into good repair and to provide basic amenities. These can include "adequate drainage facilities"

The effects are similar — but the prices vary considerably! The kitchen units illustrated opposite are budget-priced and give you a limited choice of sizes and interior fitments. Above is the luxury alternative. These are beautifully made, hand-finished and give you an almost infinite variety of dimensions and interior fittings to choose from. Below. An intermediate range of white and blue units whose prices and available choices are in between the two ranges above.

and "satisfactory facilities for preparing and cooking food" among other things.

The amounts of money handed out are strictly limited, but to find out if you qualify, how much you might get and under what conditions it would be given you, contact your Local Authority. Remember that you cannot start work until your grant has been approved.

Will you be liable for VAT?

Almost certainly. Since June 1984 VAT at the standard rate is payable on all kitchen improvements in the home. The only times you **don't** have to add on VAT are:

1. When a new kitchen is part of work in progress on a new building.

2. When a new kitchen is being created for a new self-contained flat as part of a conversion in a **listed** building.

Even so, in these circumstances, VAT is payable on all fitted electrical appliances such as built-in cookers, extractor fans, waste disposers.

The step-by-step way to achieve a new kitchen

To achieve the kitchen you want when the money available won't cover everything at once, do the work in stages. This has the advantage of giving a lot of flexibility — you can change your mind and modify your ideas in the light of experience or changing family circumstances. This sample plan that follows shows how it could be done by a young couple without children but who end up with a fully-fledged family and kitchen to go with it! It could also represent a plan of action to be followed over a few years, if money is scarce initially.

The master plan

This is what you are aiming for, so plan it as if you were going to do everything now. Lay on services in the right place and make provision for appliances. You will find adding or substituting units and appliances at a later date much simpler if you work to the increasingly standard 600mm/24in module, with the worktop 910mm/36in high and 600mm/24in (or more) deep.

The basic necessities

Sink, basic worktop and cooker are in place and all services installed. A compact refrigerator is temporarily under the worktop. Provision has been made for plumbing in dishwasher, washing-machine and waste disposer, and similarly for electric points. There is a minimum number of units — but from a range which the manufacturer guarantees he will go on producing. Most of the storage is on open shelves or hanging from the wall or ceiling. Flooring is inexpensive vinyl sheet, walls painted, and lighting in place although the fittings are inexpensive.

Midway improvements

Babies and small children impose new priorities. A washing machine (and tumble-dryer if possible) need to be added, preferably in a utility area off the main kitchen. More refrigerator space is also required, so a bigger fridge/freezer is built in or an extra freezer is added under the worktop. Closed storage is also advisable from a safety standpoint — so more units, both base and wall, are put in, and shelves enclosed. If long-term wear is going to justify a high quality floor (such as vinyl-topped cork, ceramic tiles, etc) now is the time to install it.

Finishing stages

As children grow up, the dishwasher becomes even more of a necessity. Possibly a waste disposer, also. The rest of the units can be added, possibly the original low cost worktop replaced (see pages 54-57), with tiles above. If a wall oven, plus space for a microwave, is envisaged, it can be housed beside the fridge/freezer unit, or beside the cooker which could be replaced by a hob with storage unit below. The final choice of table, chairs, light fittings can be made now and, possibly, re-decoration carried out in keeping with the new elements.

Small structural changes which can make a big difference

Not all structural changes are major undertakings. Sometimes quite small changes can make all the difference between an inconvenient kitchen and a well-planned one.

Most, however, must be carried out by an experienced builder who can advise you whether or not your plans should be checked by the local Building Control officer at your Local Authority.

Changing doors

Changing the direction a door opens — i.e. re-hanging it so it opens differently — often gives extra space. Or, reduce some of the space needed for the swing of a full door by having half-width double doors. Alternatively, consider sliding doors, if there is a space for them to slide into — they take up no space at all.

Windows into glazed doors

If you want access to the garden or simply more natural light, it is relatively easy to alter the window by dropping the sill to floor level because it is just a matter of cutting the brickwork out rather than putting in a new lintel.

Roof lights

It is not very expensive to replace a section of a sloping roof with a roof-light or Velux window (double glazed, hinged, sealed unit with its own flashing). This need not involve altering the structure of the roof.

Stealing extra space by taking down a non-structural wall

Many larders can be incorporated into the kitchen because their walls are rarely structural. If you use the newly-made space for storage units, install a ventilated air brick in the outside wall and have a cool, airy space for storing perishables like vegetables.

Knocking two small rooms into one — by taking down a non-structural wall

Many houses, both terraced and semi-detached have three not very big rooms on the ground floor. The wall between the two main ones is often non-structural and removing it can give you a large family kitchen with a utility room at the back. This opening will need a steel beam (RSJ) across the ceiling to support the floors above and will have to be checked with the local Building Control Officer. But it is a comparatively inexpensive way to obtain a much larger kitchen.

Left opposite. Stage 1: the first basics are in place, some permanently (e.g. the sink) some temporarily (e.g. the small refrigerator tucked under the worktop). Space allowed, and plumbing put in, for adding a dishwasher and washing machine later on.

Right opposite. Stage 2: the basics up-graded to cope with needs of young family: a large fridge-freezer replaces the small one; the washing machine is in place; more storage and a better quality floor have been invested in.

Right. Stage 3: the Master Plan achieved with a new island unit to take hob and provide more storage, with a lighting/extractor fan overhead. Wall ovens and a microwave slot into where the old cooker was.

Services are the sharp end of kitchen planning — the plumbing, the water supply, the drains, the electrics, the heating and hot water, the fuel supplies and the ventilation. If they all work right, the kitchen works well. If not, there's chaos.

You don't personally need to unravel the mysteries of the foul drain or the technicalities of ring mains, but it is a good thing to be aware of what is possible, what is expensive and what affects other aspects of your plan. What's more, you'll have to come to decisions about services early on in the planning of your kitchen. Decisions about gas, for instance, mean galvanising the Gas Board into action. The work has to be carried out before you install units or appliances, let alone decorate, because everything becomes much more expensive to introduce, alter or add on to at a later date.

How to check up on the plumbing

1. Is it simple and compact like this? Good plumbing layouts are as compact as possible, with short pipe runs, easily accessible drains and appliances needing a water supply sited as near to the sink as possible. This makes the plumbing cheaper to install as well as more efficient.
2. Cold water for drinking should come directly off the mains — this is normally how the cold water tap in the kitchen is supplied. Water supplies in the UK are regulated by the local Area Water Authorities, who decide how many other taps and appliances you can also run directly off the main rather than from the cold water storage tank.
3. Where there is central heating, hot water for the whole house is heated by the central heating boiler and stored in the hot water cylinder. If the boiler has to be sited in the kitchen, rather than in a nearby utility room, there are now compact, high-output boilers which can fit into a run of units, either on the floor or on the wall.
4. Alternative ways of heating water are:
i. Instantaneous gas or electric water heaters at the sink — which just heat the water as you use it.
ii. Back boilers to a coal or gas fire, stove or Aga-type cooker.
iii. Off-peak electric storage water heating — a large, extremely well-lagged cylinder with an immersion heater that is charged at off-peak times. This can be sited in the kitchen or elsewhere in the house.
5. The drains. Normally this is a 2in/50mm waste pipe from the sink, which should fall as steeply as possible to the main drain so gravity helps speed away the waste. The sink trap stops smells coming up from the drain; it can usually be unscrewed in order to clear any blockages. Where there is main drainage, your drains are your responsibility up to the point where they join up with the main sewer. If you have your own septic tank or cess-pit, the whole system is your responsibility. It is expensive to alter existing drainage patterns and worth avoiding if possible.
6. Pipework today is normally carried out in copper or plastic, the former for hot water.

7. Stopcocks are advisable at sinks and appliances which use water, so the supply can be easily shut off.
8. Plan for appliances and their plumbing even if you intend to put them in later on. It is much less expensive to cap off the pipes until they are needed than to plumb in the machine afresh when you get it.
9. If you live in a hard water area and feel strongly about soft water, you can put in a water softener, sited anywhere near where the mains supply enters the house. Keeping hot water temperatures at or above 70°C discourages the build-up of lime scale.

Elementary Electrics

1. High wattage appliances, such as electric cookers, ovens and water heaters, need their own circuit which they are permanently plugged into but you should be able to switch them off.
2. Fixed appliances, such as washing machines, dishwashers, fridges, freezers, waste disposers, etc, each need their own 13-amp socket. These sockets, on the normal ring main, should be positioned above the work surface, away from water sources.
3. In addition, also on the ring main, every kitchen needs at least four other sockets — for all the other small appliances such as the coffee machine, electric kettle, toaster and so on.
4. The lighting needs to be planned (see pages 88-91) so that the wiring and switches for the lighting circuit can be in place before the room is decorated.
5. Because electrical systems can be dangerous (many household fires start with an electrical fault) it is important to make sure all electrical work is done by qualified electricians to the specifications approved by the Institute of Electrical Engineers.
6. Voltage in the UK is 240V. Appliances designed for other voltages need transformers before being plugged in.
7. The fuses in standard modern 13-amp plugs are there to protect your appliance, so it is worth checking the manufacturer's instructions and using the correct one. As a general rule, most appliances up to a 700 watts rating use 3-amp fuses. Those with a rating above 700 watts (and some with motors like vacuum cleaners and spin driers) take 13-amp fuses.
8. The Electricity Board is responsible for all the wiring up to your meter box — you for the wiring in your house. You have a choice of tariffs: the Oridinary Tariff; the Off-peak Tariff E — which gives storage heaters an eight-hour off-peak charge at a much cheaper rate; or Economy 7 — which supplies at off-peak prices for seven hours during the night and at slightly higher than normal prices during the day.

Right: Open and shut ingenuity — these sockets are mounted on a removable panel.

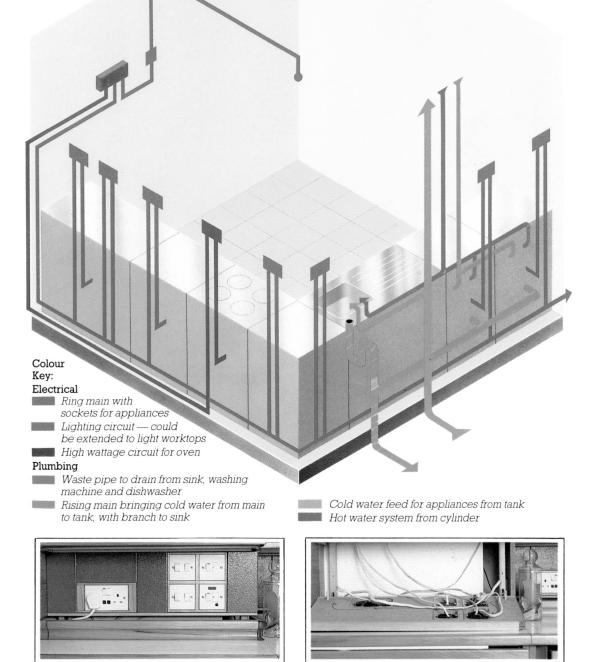

Colour
Key:
Electrical
- Ring main with sockets for appliances
- Lighting circuit — could be extended to light worktops
- High wattage circuit for oven

Plumbing
- Waste pipe to drain from sink, washing machine and dishwasher
- Rising main bringing cold water from main to tank, with branch to sink
- Cold water feed for appliances from tank
- Hot water system from cylinder

You couldn't plan a modern kitchen without electricity, but you may not want an all-electric one. Which other fuels you choose will depend on what you prefer to cook on, which you choose for heating, what is available in your area and which is most practical for you.

Cost is also a deciding factor. But remember as you do your calculations, the Government — or OPEC — can hoist the price up overnight and upset your plans.

What to cook on

There is no "best" fuel for cooking — the choice is very much a personal matter. If possible, though, it can be an advantage to have an alternative way to cook, such as an electric grill when the gas supply is cut, or a gas or electric hob when you don't want to keep the Aga going.

Getting gas: mains gas

This depends on the availability in your district of mains gas. The Local Gas Board supplies, connects (free if you're less than 10 metres from their main supply pipe), inspects, sets standards and sends bills.

Today all gas in the UK is from the North Sea — which is not toxic any more, but is still volatile, so leaks are highly dangerous.

Mains piping is increasingly made from heavy-gauge PVC. But inside the house, copper piping is now used. The cooker can be connected up with flexible piping so it can be pulled out for cleaning easily. Ideally, all pipes should be concealed but must be accessible in case of leaks. All gas appliances should carry the Gas Council's Seal of Approval.

The alternative: bottled gas

This is available anywhere but as it is generally more expensive than mains gas, it is only worth considering where there is no mains gas supply.

The gas used is Propane or Butane, which has been bottled under pressure. It is not poisonous, but like natural gas it can explode. It is delivered in various-sized cylinders depending on how much you use. Bear in mind that cylinders have to be stored outside, away from a heat source.

Most gas appliances can now be bought with burners adapted to run off bottled gas. It is even possible to run central heating and hot water for a large country house off bottled gas — suppliers only demand proper access for their delivery lorries. Look up your local supplier in the Yellow Pages under the heading "Bottled Gas".

Oil

If you plan to have an oil-fired boiler or Aga in the kitchen you will have to supply the storage tank and check with your Local Authority about any siting regulations.

It's a good idea to have as large a tank as possible so that you can take advantage of seasonal discounts. It should be situated outside as near the appliance as possible and slightly higher, as the oil travels by a gravity feed system to the appliance from the tank. However it also has to be accessible to the delivery tanker — normally not more than 100 yards from the front gate or hard standing.

Local installers and suppliers' names are in the Yellow Pages — many, but not all, have an arrangement with one of the big oil companies.

Solid fuel

This term covers coal, smokeless fuel and anthracite as well as wood, peat and dry rubbish. There are now numerous solid fuel boilers, cooking stoves, closed stoves and special grates and even re-conditioned antique stoves that can be sited in a kitchen. Of course, anything burning solid fuel needs a chimney or a special flue, so its position in the kitchen must allow for this.

The other consideration is whether you are going to link your solid fuel appliance with another, say, oil-fired one so that when it is not possible or convenient to run the solid fuel one, you have an alternative heat source. If so, the two different appliances should be sited reasonably close to each other.

All solid fuel is bulky. It needs some undercover storage near where it is to be used and a larger storage area, also under cover, further away. If your solid fuel boiler is a gravity-feed one, its hopper must be carefully sited.

Right: Traditional Aga cooker runs on gas, oil, solid fuel or electricity. Left: An Aga with boiler which also heats hot water and radiators.

The idyllic kitchen is warm in winter and cool in summer. The right balance is hard to achieve because of the heat generated by cooking. The answer is therefore a matter of combining heating with ventilation.

If you already have central heating and are re-planning the kitchen, or if there is no space for ordinary radiators, look at high-output ones which are more compact, vertical ladder-type ones, or skirting radiators. Be sure to put on adjustable valves, so you can regulate the heat if necessary.

If you have a continuously-burning cooker such as an Aga or Rayburn, it will give off a good background heat, keeping the room comfortably warm. Many will also heat radiators and/or hot water as well. A solid-fuel or wood-burning stove will perform in the same way.

An open fire is a pleasant addition to a big kitchen but, unless it has a slow-burning grate and/or heats water as well, it is too much work to rely on it to heat the room all the time.

Right: High-output gas boiler designed to fit within standard 600mm units — wall-hung or under the worktop.

Below: Elegant radiator made up of flat panels only juts out 70mm. Stove-enamelled in choice of colours — even stripes!

There should be a separate means of ventilation, independent of windows. The trouble with windows is that when opened in cold weather, too much heat is lost.

If kept open in summer, without special screens, they allow insects to come in. The solution is a modern extractor fan which will remove steam and grease and smells efficiently and, in doing so, keep the kitchen and its decorations cleaner. The best place for an extractor fan is over the cooker and the most efficient type consists of a cooker hood with a short straight duct to the outside.

Hoods without a fan or duct can only remove some of the steam and grease from the cooking, not the smells, the heat or the smoke.

Powerful extractor fans without hoods on walls or windows can also provide quite efficient ventilation and remove steam, smells and heat. They are most effective directly above the cooker — so decide on the type and location for an extractor, before siting the cooker.

Above: A cooker hood that matches wall units — you pull it out to turn it on. Effective but noisy!

Below: A revolutionary cooker hood, elegant to look at when open, invisible under wall units when shut. Electronically controlled and refreshingly quiet.

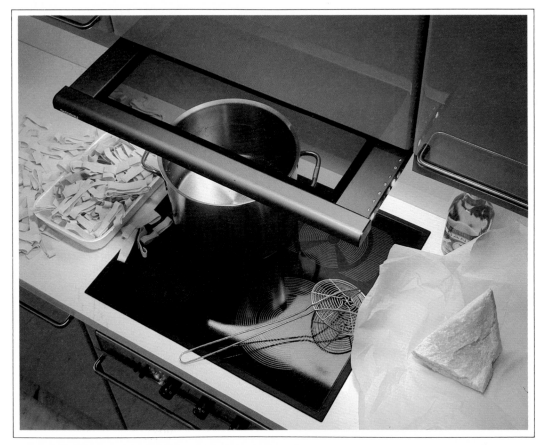

A FITTED KICHEN? OR A DIFFERENT KITCHEN?

A fitted kitchen is today's most popular solution: matching floor and wall units are carefully integrated with worktops, sink, and appliances to provide work surface, versatile storage and an integrated style. It's a solution that works well in the tiniest spaces as well as the largest rooms — for which some manufacturers have also designed chairs, tables and bookshelves. Fitted kitchens are what the kitchen manufacturers, planners and shops are so successful in selling!

Before you order a fitted kitchen, however, it is worth making quite sure that it is indeed the solution for your kitchen. There are alternatives. Some are as, if not more, expensive than buying a complete fitted kitchen. But many are much cheaper.

Right and below: A specially designed kitchen — in this case there's not a unit in sight. Illustrated is one of Johnny Grey's Alternative Kitchens, individually designed for a particular client. He prefers to design large pieces of furniture to provide storage, work surfaces, sink and fridge housing, etc.

If you want a kitchen like this specially designed and made for you, it will be a one-off job and almost certainly an expensive one.

• The High Tech solution. The original idea behind High Tech was to use industrial and commercial equipment for domestic purposes. Some of these items, because designed for professional use, will function much more efficiently than those designed specifically for home use. Another element is the finding of new uses for humble objects and materials, so High Tech is an exercise in ingenious recycling as well.

The first person to create a complete High Tech house (in the sense that he used mass-produced materials, and construction methods normally reserved for factories) was the designer Charles Eames, as long ago as 1949.

The ideas simmered among the avant garde, only surfacing into general public awareness in the 1970s.

In terms of kitchen design many aspects of High Tech have had a good influence. Materials (stainless steel, industrial ceramic tiles, studded rubber flooring) are chosen because they are exceptionally hard-wearing and easy to clean. Appliances such as restaurant cookers, professional cooking tools, storage on wheels (you roll it where you need it) and easy to clean stainless steel or plastic-coated racking systems all make kitchen work easier.

The recycling element adds the fun — and the clichés! Tractor-seat chairs, dinette-style tables (clamped to the floor), graph paper graphics, laboratory glass, factory light fittings are all recognizable elements.

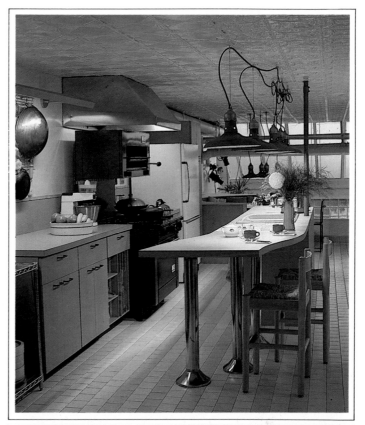

Above: High tech in full flower — note the spartan wall and floor treatment, the dinette-style worktop, the industrial "goose-neck" light fittings, restaurant-size cooker with matching hood and wire-grid trolley.
Below: not obviously High Tech, but indebted to it in its functional simplicity and its trolley-wheeled oven and storage.

Some of the most interesting and original kitchens are those which have been improvised. Their owners have wanted something not generally available, perhaps, and have had to work out their own solutions. Or, very often, a strict budget has led to ingenious ways of making the most of relatively inexpensive raw materials.

There are several starting points from which you can create your alternative kitchen:
• Converting old furniture. Old pine chests, cupboards and washstands can be altered to take sinks and even hobs. Use old dressers for their original purposes — to store china and cutlery. Old doors can be stripped of their paint and cut to size to make cabinet parts. Using old pine in this way is a sympathetic way to modernise a kitchen in a period house or old cottage. Avoid new reproduction pieces, which are often rather brash. Choose old pieces with a soft pleasing patina. These are no longer cheap, but the total cost of a kitchen made from them can be less than a complete new fitted kitchen.
• The no-unit solution. This is the simplest and cheapest alternative for anyone who can do enough carpentry to make a framework which can hold up a sink and worktop, with a shelf beneath. With cooking and serving equipment carefully chosen and imaginatively arranged the effect is simple but stylish.

• Your own design. Whether carried out by yourself or with the help of local craftsmen this gives you a custom-made kitchen without the cost of a custom designer. Even at today's rates a good carpenter can produce exactly what you want cheaper than you could buy it ready-made, especially if you have inexpensive raw materials to hand, such as old pine doors to cut down.
• Your own design from ready-mades. Make up your own fitted kitchen from ready-made standard carcases. Choose your own doors — they can be made from laminates of your own choice. Or use old doors, fabric stretched on a frame, Georgian wired glass within a wood frame. You can also get the interior fittings separately.

Below: A unique kitchen island with hob, storage and three sinks. The sinks have been hollowed out of a single solid piece of teak, like sinks in the butler's pantry of old. The owner did the marbling and stencilling round the sides herself.

Right: Recycled doors on new units echo the simple period style of the house and complement the brick floor.

Even tiny spaces can be made into viable kitchens — but the smaller the space, the more careful and precise the planning needs to be.

Planning guidelines discussed earlier (pages 16-17) for kitchens in general — work sequence, worktop heights, storage space and so on — apply just as much if not more when you want to turn a small space into somewhere to prepare, cook and clear up meals.

The first, most important decision to make is about the sort of meals you want to be able to prepare.

In a small space there are invariably limitations on what can be cooked and for how many people. A mini-kitchen does not easily lend itself to family living! But, with ingenuity, you can entertain in style. (See the small but elegant kitchen on page 11.)

The secret is to be ruthless and, having decided realistically what you will attempt, work out the absolute minimum equipment you will need.

Could this be as little as the legendary Cordon Bleu discipline of a sharp knife, a fork and a wooden spoon? Probably not! But this is the time to invest in dual and triple purpose storage, cooking and serving dishes, stacking china and versatile glasses. Also to throw out (or store elsewhere) everything not in use at least once a week.

Services to plan for

Every mini-kitchen, like every kitchen, needs some basic services. A hot and cold water supply, connection to the waste and electric points are essential. You can usually get away with only a 13-amp power supply for a refrigerator and two-ring hob, instead of the special high-amp circuit needed by normal ovens and cookers. You will also need effective and flexible lighting.

How mini?

If you have a run 3m/10ft long with space above (for storage) and below (for appliances) you can plan an effective all-purpose kitchen. This can often turn out to be more convenient than a much larger one which has been less well planned.

Where there is less space, you need more ingenuity. Pioneers of equipment for small spaces are the boat and caravan manufacturers. It is well worth seeing just how much they manage to cram into minuscule corners. Also, where electricity is a problem, what can be done with calor gas.

The kitchen from the leastest

The barest minimum, if you are to do more than boil a kettle, needs a space just wide enough to accommodate a small sink set into a worktop with room underneath for the plumbing and a small refrigerator. This would be around 75cm/2ft 6in. You would also need several electric points because any "cooking" would have to be done by boiling kettles, plugging in electric frying pans or slow-cook-pots. You would also have to plan for storage.

Ready-made mini-kitchens

Several manufacturers make these packages which offer various combinations in one unit. For instance, you can have a sink, draining board and two electric rings with a continuous worktop in stainless steel. Under the sink is a cupboard and beside it (under the electric rings and drainer) a refrigerator. Alternatively, a sink/dishwasher or sink/fridge/hob combination is available.

They are not, yet, things of beauty, but fit into a space only 1m/3ft 3in across and about 60cm/2ft deep (depending how far the cooker controls and cupboard handles stick out).

Minis to your own specifications

In many ways it is more satisfactory to invent your own mini-kitchen and build it into the space yourself. As well as the sink, worktop, cooking rings and refrigerator, you may want to add other things. For instance, a portable convection oven or microwave, a cooker hood (to provide some

Left: Minimal walk-in kitchen. U-shaped plan makes the most of space available. Units, cupboards and appliances line the walls.

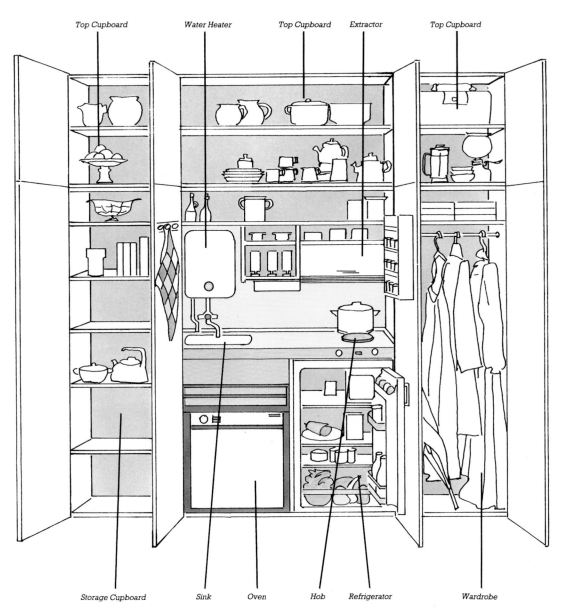

Top Cupboard   Water Heater   Top Cupboard   Extractor   Top Cupboard

Storage Cupboard   Sink   Oven   Hob   Refrigerator   Wardrobe

Above: Blueprint for a mini-kitchen plus a lot of well-planned storage. This one has been designed to fit into a space only 2m/6ft 6in across, 600mm/2ft deep and 2.5m/8ft high.

invaluable really effective ventilation), a waste disposer, a mini-freezer, an extra pull-out worktop.

You can also design the overall effect so it fits in with the rest of the house/room.

A small amount of extra space for storage can be used to great advantage. The back of a door can be fitted up so it holds almost as much as a cupboard. Grid systems and wire baskets can turn wasted space between shelves and on side walls into usable storage.

It is always more convenient if there is some way to shut off a mini-kitchen when it is not in use. Doors, if there is space, are best because of the additional scope for storage they offer. Fold-back doors, specially hinged down the middle as well as at each side, take only half the floor space to open. Blinds, from floor to ceiling, take up no floor space at all, but give you no storage possibilities either.

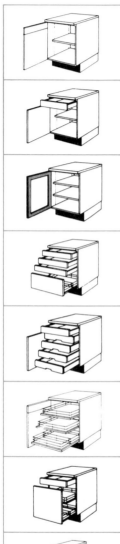

Inside every modern unit is its carcase. The carcase provides the rigid structure as well as supporting shelves, drawers and all you put in them. If units are worth buying, they must have good quality carcases.

Points to look for in a carcase

1 Rigid construction — sides and shelves with a minimum thickness of 15mm/⅝in, the back 4mm/ ³⁄₁₆in.

2 Every surface laminated. Visible edges in choice of colour to match doors.

3 Firm joints — not screws in plastic plugs.

4 Provision for adjusting shelf level. Bonus if unused holes can be covered.

5 Dust seal round doors and drawers — sadly only one manufacturer offers this at present.

6 Strong hinges which open more than 90°, and can be adjusted so they hang properly.

7 Magnetic doors which close automatically after a certain point.

8 Adjustable legs for units to stand on — important when floors aren't level.

9 Base plinth held on by magnetic catches.

10 Drawers: one-piece injection moulded drawers are best, lighter, and easier to keep clean. Alternatively, separate liners can be fitted.

11 Smooth running drawers — the newest run on ball bearings in telescopic runners which are concealed under the drawer to prevent dust, crumbs, etc, fouling them.

12 Strength — one maker tests drawers to take loads up to 12kg/28lbs. Pull-outs to take 40kg/ 90lbs. Full-height larder units to take 200kg/ 450lbs.

13 Drawer stop — to prevent you inadvertently pulling the drawer right out.

14 What are carcases made from? Today the big manufacturers almost invariably use a material with a core of chipboard or some other man-made composite which is then laminated with melamine on both sides. This is used for bases, sides and shelving of units — doors, too, sometimes. This board is more stable than natural wood and for its price makes a stronger, more rigid, more stable carcase. Only wood carcases made by quality manufacturers producing high quality one-off kitchens can match these.

Points to look for in choosing units

● Choice of widths — top makers give you units in 12 different widths.

● Variety — so you get the drawer, shelf, cupboard combinations you need. Also housings for cookers, ovens, dishwashers, fridges, etc.

● Good ideas to simplify storage, such as deep drawers for pans, larder units etc.

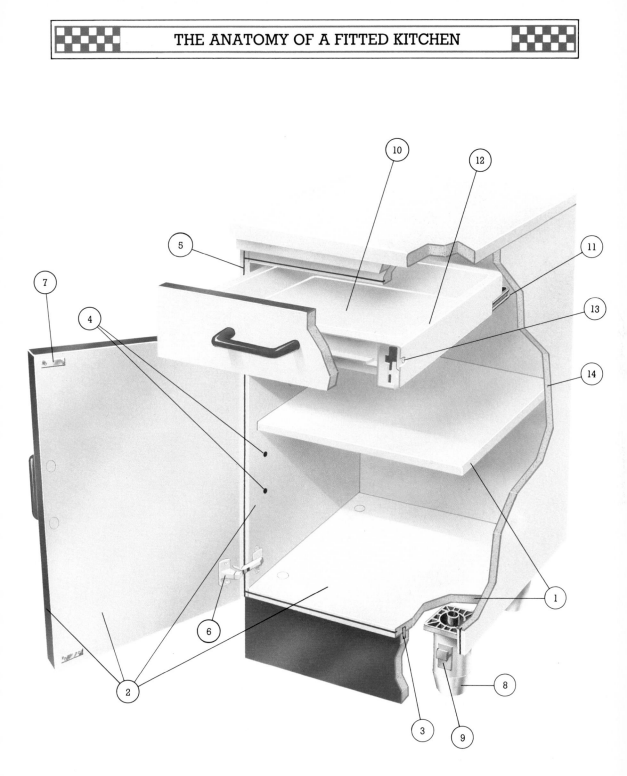

Above: What to look for in a well-constructed unit; numbers refer to the list opposite.
Left: 20 of the variations on a basic base unit offered by Siematic who make nearly 100 different base unit carcases and offer a choice of over 50 door finishes!

Natural wood looks good in almost every style of kitchen. It is the material traditionally used for cupboards, dressers and tables and although there are now alternatives, wood is still such a popular choice that nearly every manufacturer makes at least one range of wood-fronted units. Oak — pale, dark or smoky, veneered, profiled or stained — leads the field. But pine, ash, alder, beech, walnut, birch, elm, cherry, maple — you name it, unit doors are made from it!

Each different type of wood gives a slightly different effect and this can be emphasised by the way it is used. For instance, some fronts are designed like nineteenth-century doors with intricate profiled frames. Some are utterly plain, others discreetly slatted. Dark-stained oak, heavily profiled, usually with a name like Breton or Saratoga, will create a prosperous farmhouse look, that marries well with traditional tiles and pottery. But if it is not to be overwhelming, this needs a big kitchen. Light oak, birch or any of the paler woods give a kitchen a cooler, crisper, more contemporary feel. New pine is unpretentious. Antique pine, converted into unit doors, blends very well in a sympathetic conversion of a period house.

Below: New pine, carefully treated, can look as mellow as old pine. These solid wood doors have a discreet square profile. The wood itself has a soft, golden finish. As a result, these units would blend sympathetically into a period house (or a modern kitchen extension to one) and set off genuine antiques — such as the quilted tablecloth, chairs and lamp here.

Wood, of course, is always comparatively expensive. The more solid wood there is in a unit door, the more expensive it will be. Costs can be cut if you opt for a veneer rather than the solid wood, or a solid wood frame round a veneer panel. Veneers are now so convincing that it is sometimes hard to tell just how a door has been constructed and what of. The brochure might give you a clue; here the rule is, like sandy beaches in the holiday brochures, if it isn't mentioned, it isn't there.

The advantage of solid wood is that, properly seasoned and made up, it will last, can be sanded, renovated, stripped and re-polished — whereas once a veneer, however well-made, starts chipping only a skilled craftsman can bring it back to life.

Solid wood and veneers which show off the natural colour and grain of the wood usually have a clear lacquer or polyurethane seal — which is practical to keep clean. Wood which has only been wax polished is very attractive, but in practice takes up greasy marks every time it is touched and needs regular, careful cleaning and re-waxing.

Below: Solid oak doors and cupboards can range in colour from pale bleached blond to an almost Jacobean black. These dark units give a farmhouse atmosphere to this spacious kitchen. The solid wood doors are carved in a traditional Norman pattern, as are the barley-sugar shelf supports. Behind the solid façades are high-quality modern carcases, complete with the most sophisticated storage fittings.

Wood is extremely versatile, but if a natural wood kitchen is not what you want, consider one of the many possible variations.

One increasingly popular treatment is to paint or stain wood. Staining shows up the natural grain, but adds colour or tone. Black stained wood is a favourite in high tech schemes. Many manufacturers make ready-stained unit fronts, but it is not difficult to do yourself. As the graining will show, the wood you stain must be of a consistent quality.

Painting wood fronts has long been a way of disguising doors made from inferior or poorly-matched wood. It can be straightforward — to add colour or just to protect the wood. Or it can be a work of art. Now that the old techniques of dragging, spattering, marbling, stencilling and lacquering are being revived, each kitchen can be a unique creation. Do it yourself, if you have confidence but no money, or commission a talented professional to do it for you, if you have less skill but more money. Some manufacturers already offer hand-painted, hand-dragged, hand-finished ranges of high quality.

An alternative way of getting some of the warmth of wood but more variety of colour and texture is to choose door fronts with contrasting panelling inside a wood frame. Or simply with well-designed wood handles. Partnered with other natural materials in the panels, like rattan, wood weaves or plaited bamboo, these unit doors can look as elegant as the best all-wood ones and are particularly good for the unkitcheny kitchen as they look less obviously like kitchen furnishing than most all-wood or

Above: Wood customised with delicate painting and an Art Deco stencil on unit doors. This treatment works out expensive when professionally painted, but amateurs can spend talent to get equally exciting effects.

plastic laminate ones. Usually the panelling inside the wood frame is a plastic laminate of one sort or another. This has the great advantage of making them a lot cheaper!

Below: Plain paint, if it's in a pretty colour, can provide the key to a decorative scheme for a whole kitchen and living area.

Above: These kitchen units were custom-made in knotty pine over 10 years ago, which had darkened unattractively. They have been given new life with paint — pale beige dragged over an even paler undercoat.

Kitchen units with plastic laminate fronts come in an increasing number of colours, textures and designs. Some of the most effective kitchen schemes are based on plastic laminate units. Their main drawback is that as techniques of printing plastic laminates improves and the imitation of natural materials and textures becomes more realistic, the temptation to produce cheap imitations is strong. Not just wood or linen, but even the heavily profiled doors and drawer fronts from the most expensive ranges are now being moulded and pressed into plastic laminate. The secret of success is to avoid plastic laminates that try to pass themselves off as something else: wood or marble, for instance. Select those that are unashamedly laminates for the qualities they offer.

Colour is one of the most attractive things about plastic laminates. The colours can be brilliant — especially in the ranges with a high-gloss lacquer finish. The all-white kitchen is sparked into life with a brilliant primary colour used as a stripe or handle on the door front.

Good quality laminates, like the now standard carcases, have a number of advantages over second-rate wood. They are stable and won't warp; they are extremely easy to keep clean and look good for a long time; and they are very reasonably priced for the most part.

These pictures illustrate the way the same white laminate units can be the basis of a number of very different colour schemes and types of kitchen.

Right above. A bright, crisp cheerful red and white kitchen. The red handles on the units match up with the red ceiling, shelves, table and chairs and set off the white units with great style.

Right below. This scheme shows how white units can be the basis of an informal kitchen look. In this predominantly white kitchen, the food and wood, fruits and plants provide natural colour, and the green floor and ceiling provide a sympathetic and restful background.

Below. This kitchen uses a bold clear yellow to partner and dominate the white. The yellow of the handles, cooker hood, shelves, chairs, wall, floor and blind creates a sunny family kitchen which looks sophisticated, too.

The old fashioned kitchen dresser is the forerunner of another approach to storage: the display-it-all technique. Display has several advantages. Everything is visible, so you can see it when you need it without peering into drawers and cupboards. A lot of kitchen equipment — utensils and stores as well as pretty china and handsome pans — is visually interesting. Effective displays often contribute greatly to the impact of some of the most imaginative kitchens. Finally, it's nearly always cheaper to put up shelves, even to buy an old dresser, than to achieve the equivalent storage area in new ready-made units. Nearly every kitchen has a judicious mix of storage — as had the old dressers with their shelves above and drawers and cupboards below. It takes an obsessively tidy lifestyle to do without cupboards altogether, but even the unit manufacturers recognise the need to break up the monotonous row of doors and offer a variety of shelves, spice racks and open midway units so you can vary their kitchens according to your own taste. The major disadvantage of open storage is that grease and dust accumulate over the years and everything needs to be cleaned regularly, which can be tedious.

The Island Store

Free-standing units in kitchens can be treated just like large base units with storage concealed behind cupboard doors. Or they can provide specialised — and often decorative — storage space for things you need when using the island. If, for instance, the island has a hob fitted into its worktop, then pans and cooking implements need to be stored nearby — a rack with pans and tools hanging down from it is practical and looks effective. (The rack itself can be suspended from the ceiling along with necessary lighting and extractor fan.) If the island has a sink for preparing vegetables, then the vegetables, parers and peelers and the invaluable food processor can all be stored on the island. If the island is primarily a chopping surface with cross-grained wood worktop, a special knife holder could be incorporated. Butcher's blocks are really mini-islands — some come with drawers and racks. Others are moveable trolleys and can be tucked away neatly under a worktop when not in use.

Above. The kitchen dresser principle — open shelf storage above and below worktop displays cooking things and china.

Below. Specially-designed island work station with cross-grained chopping surface, towel rail, vegetable and cutlery drawers, and extra storage underneath.

Opposite. Old butcher's block mounted on a table to make a mini-island. Note slot for safe knife storage.

How many shelves, units or cupboards?

Before you fill your kitchen with units, it pays to work out exactly how much and what kind of storage you need and where it will be most convenient.

Making your inventory

Nobody has the same storage needs and as most kitchen storage problems arise because there are too many things and too little space, your first task is to make an inventory of everything you need to store. Then eliminate as much as possible! Why keep pans so damaged that they burn food? Why keep china that is cracked and chipped or the remnants of a set you never liked? Or empty jam jars when you haven't made jam for five years? Throw them out! Storage space is too valuable to house things you neither need nor use. You may be able to minimise equipment by choosing appliances and pans with more than one function (see pages 68-69).

Many items could perhaps be moved out of the kitchen altogether, for instance, the "best" china, or glass that is only used occasionally. If there's space, cleaning and laundry equipment could be housed in a separate utility area — see pages 94-95. Simple adjustments like this leave more room for things in everyday use, and could mean you need less expensive storage than you thought.

Where to store what

Obviously, the most convenient arrangement is to keep each item as near as possible to the place where it is going to be used — cooking implements near the stove, for instance. So try to keep this commonsense principle in mind.

Near the sink

You need a lot of storage space near the sink because it is the focal point of the work triangle and the centre of so many activities related to preparing or clearing up a meal. Space in this area is required for:
1. Items needed for the preparation of food such as knives, chopping boards, strainers, colanders, saucepans, and any specialised tools for preparing fruit and vegetables.
2. Washing up equipment, such as brushes and scourers, plate racks (over the draining board) or the dishwasher (plumbed in under it). Everyday china, cutlery and glass can either be stored near the sink (to make putting it away after washing up easier) or near where you normally eat (to simplify laying the table).
3. Cleaning supplies used everyday, such as the various detergents for washing up and for the dishwasher, the floor and the windows (but put your bulk supplies elsewhere); plus brushes, buckets and cloths used for "wet" cleaning jobs like the floor.
4. A small container for wet rubbish (vegetable peelings, etc) under the sink.

Near the cooker/preparation/mixing area

Everything needed for cooking should be stored near the cooker (or hob and oven). This includes food processors, mixers or small whisking appliances, as well as stores like flour, sugar, salt, pepper, herbs and spices. If you boil the kettle for cups of tea or coffee on the stove, the mugs, tea, coffee and sugar also need to be kept nearby. If you have an electric kettle all this can be elsewhere, but still together. Either way, the kettle has to be filled at the sink, and the milk fetched from the refrigerator.

Near the serving area

This area is the link between where you cook and where you eat and is often to one side of the cooker. It is the ideal place to store serving dishes and the food you put on the table without further preparation such as jams, sauces, breakfast cereals, biscuits etc.

High or low level storage?

In an ideal world, all storage would be placed so that no stretching up or bending down would be necessary. In reality, as there is never room for everything to be stored at worktop height, many things have to be stored less conveniently — at a higher or lower level. High-level storage is best used for the comparatively light things used less frequently, so that if you do have to reach them by standing on a stool, they are easy to lift down.

New developments are making low-level storage much more accessible (see pages 52-53). This is the best place for heavy things like big casseroles.

The bare minimum

The chart below shows the amount of storage space recommended by the Department of Environment for the average household. It includes everything except the fridge and whatever they define as "laundry equipment and supplies". How do your needs compare? Will you need more or less storage?

Units needed by a 1/2 person household (to be increased proportionately for larger households)
Wall units: 4 × 600mm/24in plus 1 × 400mm/16in
Base units: 3 × 600mm/24in plus 1 × 400mm/16in

Units needed by a 3/4 person household
Wall units: 5 × 600mm/24in plus 1 × 300mm/12in
Base units: 4 × 600mm/24in plus 1 × 400mm/16in

Above: The ideal cutlery drawer — wide and shallow so everything is seen at a glance. Here well-positioned near dishwasher and eating area.

How one family stores it all — including the cat's requirements

Left. The complete view of the Shaws' kitchen.

Centre row left. Baking dishes where you need them — under the hob. Shallower top drawer means big and small pans can be stored without wasted space.

Centre row centre. Cleaning supplies stored together on a fold-down panel under the sink so that everything can be reached without stooping, bending, groping or kneeling.

Centre row right. Stores for baking and cooking are kept near pull-down scales and above mixer, which is housed under the worktop.

Bottom row left. Often-wasted corner space has a useful carousel for chopping boards (below) and knives, choppers, etc (above).

Bottom row centre. The same corner with carousel unit closed. Even the plinth has fitted pull-out drawers, so not one inch of space is wasted.

Bottom row right. The Shaws' cats enjoy peace and protected eating space in a base drawer which can be shut out of sight after feeding time.

When choosing a new fitted kitchen you can waste a lot of money on units if you don't plan their interiors first, in order to make the most of their expensive space. Properly planned units are not only more convenient but actually create more space at comfortably-reached levels.

Some of the newer developments which have made kitchen storage more accessible and efficient in this way are:

The pull-out principle

Drawers, deep shelves which pull out from base units and tall larders all use the filing cabinet principle of easy access. Instead of bending and groping to reach things on the lowest shelves, you pull out the drawer and easily see and reach what is there, often viewing the contents from both sides! The runners are continually being improved; the best are silent, smooth running and very strong.

Almost everything can be stored in this way, from cutlery and pans, crockery and serving dishes to stores, wine and French bread!

No more "dead" corners

Carousels which either turn to bring things at the back round to the front, or emerge automatically when you open the door, can be fitted into wall or base corner units, so these are no longer dark, forgotten dumping grounds. What's more, carousels are now strongly made and solid enough to hold pans without sagging, so don't accept flimsy wire contraptions.

Above: Extra storage created at the back of a deep worktop to take small electrical appliances, or even bread! A typical midway unit.

Storage on doors

Racks on the inside of cupboard doors, or even an inner door made of wire shelving, provide extra accessible shelf space for small, light items such as spices, pan lids, etc.

Organising more space inside units

Create more space by choosing units with adjustable shelves or racks which fit under the shelves so there is as little wasted space as possible. Fitted containers often provide a compact way to keep everyday basic stores accessible.

Using the midway space

With a deeper than normal worktop midway units, designed to go between wall and base units, can either conceal appliances, coffee-making equipment or basic stores behind doors or else display them attractively.

Fold-away storage

Folding mechanisms can be used to stow food processors out of the way under the worktop until needed. Extra work surfaces, tables or ironing boards can also fold away into base units; in some ranges even the space behind the plinth can be utilised — for storing a small ladder, for instance.

Ideas like these, although first introduced by designers and manufacturers in the more expensive ranges, are quickly picked up. Special fitments soon become available, so that DIY enthusiasts can use them to upgrade very basic units inexpensively. Mail-order catalogues are an excellent source of these fittings.

Three space-savers: a pull-out table (left); fold-away storage for a mixer (below left); full-height pull-out larder (below).

Pull-out larders

The pull-out larder/storecupboard is a dramatically successful innovation. The entire contents are revealed, nothing gets lost at the back and everything is within easy reach. De luxe versions come full-height, or with the bottom section as pull-out drawers. There is also often a choice of widths. The grandest are so strongly made that the makers specify they can carry loads up to 450lb/200 kg. DIY versions are less sophisticated and need a certain amount of skill to fit satisfactorily, but are effective alternatives at a much lower cost.

Choosing a worktop

Only your kitchen floor has to take more punishment than your worktop. And, like flooring, the material chosen for the worktop is a key element in the look and style of the whole kitchen. It must complement the units and affects (and is affected by) your choice of sink, taps, hob and cooker. A hard-wearing continuous worktop is important in a kitchen in several ways.

• It helps the work flow more efficiently, as anyone who has struggled with only a sink and drainer and the top of a waist-high refrigerator for a worktop will tell you. In fact, the continuous work surface is yet another of the invaluable ideas which originated from the Bauhaus designers in the 1920s.

• It creates a feeling of more space, especially if sinks and hobs are inset into the worktop rather than interrupting it. For the same reason a marble square for pastry making or a heat-resistant tile beside the cooker for hot pans are often better as inset panels than as different worktop sections.

• A continuous worktop can unify what might otherwise be an odd collection of appliances, shelves and cupboards. A new continuous worktop will give a run of old units a dramatic face-lift, and is often a comparatively simple way of renovating a kitchen without going to the expense of new units.

Materials for worktops

The ideal material for a worktop would be one which withstands any amount of water, would be be easy to keep clean, could be chopped on without marking or blunting your knife or damaging the worktop itself, be heat-resistant, non-staining and always smooth and cool for pastry-making. Not surprisingly, no one material combines all these virtues. All sorts of materials have been tried, even studded rubber flooring. The best you can do is to find the most functional material within your price range. Below, the pros and cons of the most readily available worktops are analysed.

Plastic laminate worktops

In the end most people choose one of the plastic laminates. They are tough, practical and resist moisture, grease, stains, detergents and moderate heat. Very hot pans will mark them and very sharp knives will score them — they are not for chopping on. Prices vary according to quality, but usually plastic laminate works out to be one of the cheaper alternatives. There is also an enormous choice of colours, textures and qualities, including some convincing look-alikes for wood, marble, tiles and polished granite.

What is plastic laminate? It is fine sheets of laminate bonded on to a man-made composite board. Worktop quality laminate is extra tough, scratch resistant and non-slip. (Ordinary laminated boards sold in DIY shops for shelving are not tough enough for worktops.) Plastic

Above. Handsome, practical worktop and breakfast bar specially shaped from solid maple-strip.

Opposite. Striking tile splash-back adds art deco glamour to stainless steel sink and worktop.

laminate worktops come either with squared-off laminated edges, or set within a wood frame. Postformed worktops have a rounded front edge which looks as if it has curled in on itself. New worktops can be ordered, with or without units, from kitchen shops, department stores with kitchen departments or other stockists; each order is usually made to measure.

Solid wood

A traditional work surface, the butcher's block is made from sections of wood cut across the grain and glued together. It is still the best surface for chopping on as it is non-slip and preserves the edges of knives. Unfortunately wooden worktops are a rarity in the world of unit manufacturers. "Mini parquet" or "beech strip", found in the more expensive ranges, has a genuine wood surface, but a thin one, and, in fact, has been mounted on to the usual man-made composite base. Maple strip, however, is solid wood and when ordered from a specialist firm may only be a little more expensive than a top quality plastic laminate. You can make your own worktop of course. Woodyards will cut and plane boards to order which can then be glued and cramped to make the depth of worktop needed. Hard woods such as teak, maple and iroko need only occasional oiling to maintain and protect them. Soft woods, such as pine, need many coats of polyurethane seal to protect them from water, heat, stains, etc. This protective seal will need to be renewed from time to time.

Ceramic tiles

Well-chosen tiles can upgrade the appearance of any kitchen and there are now tiles to go with any kind of unit and every style of decoration. Not all tiles (certainly not thin wall tiles) are tough enough for worktops. Only vitrified ceramic tiles and mosaics will do. Some floor and quarry tiles might also be suitable, but most of these are quite thick and difficult to support properly. The right tiles are long-lasting, stain-resistant, don't deteriorate in contact with water and are easy to keep clean. But they must be properly laid and their grouting kept in good condition. To avoid the inevitable ugly discoloration of white grout that occurs after a while, tint the grout to match or contrast with the tiles. Epoxy grout is more difficult to apply but much more durable than the traditional kind; it can also be tinted. Tiles need a rigid and stable base, such as blockboard. Many manufacturers provide a base for tiles to go on and can supply an optional wood frame, too. The disadvantages of tiles are that anything dropped on them invariably breaks, individual tiles can crack under a sharp impact or excessive heat, and that chopping boards are an essential extra. The price of tiles varies widely and professional laying — essential unless you are experienced at tiling — can be expensive.

Stainless steel

Work surfaces in stainless steel are widely used in commercial kitchens because they are so practical, functional and hygienic. The only disadvantage for the cook is that it cannot be chopped on as it both marks easily and blunts the knife. But use of this material, apart from sinks and draining boards, in the home kitchen is limited. It is not generally offered as an alternative by kitchen unit manufacturers. It has to be ordered separately and made by a specialist firm. You can specify a flat, ribbed or textured worktop, and even order it complete in one piece with whatever size sink you want. For some the look of stainless steel throughout a kitchen is too functional, too institutional and not warm and welcoming enough. It is also an expensive material, certainly costing more than plastic laminate or maple strip.

Corian

This is a new miracle material from Du Pont, technically described as a "filled polymer", and is accordingly high-priced. But it most nearly approaches the single ideal worktop material. Corian looks like marble — either a plain milky white or a shaded pastel. But unlike real marble, it won't stain, is non-porous, won't burn and can be worked like wood. You can get a worktop of

Below. Polished granite is the sophisticated, man-made — but expensive — alternative to marble. Polished to a handsome high-gloss finish, it's harder-wearing than marble and doesn't stain yet still looks "natural".

any size and shape in Corian and it can even be made into a one-piece worktop and sink(s). If it does get damaged, it can be repaired by gently rubbing it with the finest wire wool. So it is the only worktop (apart from butcher's block wood) which lets you chop on it. The main disadvantage of Corian is its expense, so most people who buy it usually protect it from the ravages of the knife by using a wooden chopping board.

Marble
The natural luxury worktop, marble lasts forever, tolerates water and heat and keeps wonderfully cool, hence its famous assets for the pastry-maker. But otherwise it is not terribly practical, as, being slightly porous, it stains if acids like lemon juice or wine are spilt on it, and needs loving, careful maintenance to keep it looking good (scrubbing with soap, then polishing with a fine abrasive powder to restore the shine). All marble is expensive and has to be ordered from a specialist firm. Cutting, shaping and polishing marble isn't a DIY job either. Many people who hanker after marble in the kitchen settle for the much less expensive compromise of having a relatively small slab inset into their worktop.

Below. The natural combination of glossy dark slate and well-crafted wood. The thick slate worktop has been pierced to take sink and hob in contrasting stainless steel and is also used for the splashback where it is ideal for writing messages and shopping lists.

Polished granite
This is another "natural" material, favoured for elegant kitchens on the Continent. It is not actually a slice of granite, but is made from chippings of natural granite set into an epoxy resin, then cut to shape and polished. It has all the good qualities of marble but not the drawbacks of being affected by acids or heat. However it is an expensive work surface and although it features on the lists of the top German and Italian unit manufacturers, it would probably be a little less expensive to order it direct from a supplier.

Slate
Slate was the traditional farmhouse answer to marble as it didn't have to be imported from abroad at great expense. It occurs naturally in Great Britain and is still quarried in Wales and Cumbria so although expensive, it is more affordable than marble. It is also more practical, having many of the virtues of marble (keeps cool, is very tough and long-lasting) but being non-porous, it doesn't stain so easily. Slate comes in a variety of greens and blues and greys, depending on where it was quarried. It looks very handsome both in sophisticated kitchens with glossy white units as well as in rugged country kitchens with flagstone floors and natural wood furniture. It needs little or no maintenance, but a little linseed oil rubbed in occasionally will preserve its sheen.

The Work Centre approach

Once a sink was a sink was a sink: a single spout mixer tap was a big deal and which side to have your draining board was a major decision.

Sinks are now presented as "Work Centres" and both sinks and taps have style, colour and character. Choosing a sink has become more complicated but it is also much more fun because it now makes a positive contribution to the look and feel of a kitchen.

The new concept of the sink as a Work Centre means you are encouraged to use the sink more intensively. With the drainers, sink baskets and chopping boards which are available as extras, the sink becomes part of the work surface as well as the place where you wash the vegetables and the dishes. It's even more useful if a waste disposer is fitted in the second sink to dispose of rubbish.

At the same time the sink has become smaller — one of the original compact designs is only 965mm/3ft approx by 500mm/1ft 8in. This makes it possible to have a continuous run of sink, work surface and cooker in a line less than 2800mm/10ft long (see pages 16-17).

There are several decisions to make about the kind of sink you want.

What colour?

This will determine what material the sink is made from. If you want bright primary colours, black or white, a pastel shade or one of the earthy colours, it will have to be made of vitreous enamelled steel. If possible, go for the best quality you can afford because the cheaper versions will chip more readily. Many Continental firms not only offer a big colour choice but can match the sink to taps and hobs — even refrigerators and ovens occasionally.

Otherwise, there is the ever-practical stainless steel, still the most hard-wearing material. This can also match taps and hobs. Or you may choose luxurious Corian, or the latest composite, Sylac, or stick to traditional fireclay, none of which match up with hobs, etc.

What shape and size?

The new sinks come in such a variety of shapes and sizes — round or square equal-sized pairs, one big and one little, with or without drainer — that you can get almost any combination you can think of. In any case, two sinks are better than one and essential if you want to have a waste disposer. Ideally, one of your sinks should be big enough to accommodate the oven trays and biggest pans and for this reason one sink should probably be rectangular. However, people who fall in love with circular sinks find they manage somehow.

The separate vegetable washing sink, so long an enviable feature in luxury kitchens, is not necessary if you have two sinks and a waste disposer. However it *is* worth having a separate sink for laundry — see pages 94-95.

Draining boards and plate racks

If you plan to have a dishwasher, large areas of draining board are not necessary, certainly not the double drainers of old. But a small one is essential if you don't want your worktop covered in water much of the time, because there are always some things to wash up that won't fit into the dishwasher.

Drainers now come in as many shapes, sizes and colours as the new sinks they are designed to match. For efficient draining you need a

Below: One of the new Work Centres in practical stainless steel.

Above: All-blue — sink and taps match perfectly.

Below: All-white — made from Sylac, a new scratch-, stain-, heat- and impact-resistant synthetic, whose colours run throughout the material.

sloping ribbed surface of some sort: glasses, for instance, can't drain properly on a flat surface. A new idea is for the drainer also to have its own waste outlet.

If you decide not to have a dishwasher, then you not only need a generous draining board of some sort, but also a plate rack to drain and store much of your everyday china and dishes. Of course it has to be placed over the draining board and this has to be large enough to catch all the drips. Some work centre sinks come with a draining basket which you can rinse everything in and leave it to drain.

Inset or not?

Sinks are now usually designed to fit on top of, rather than underneath, the worktop. Improved and patented methods now make this type of joint more hygienic and waterproof than under-the-worktop joins.

Sinks that fit over an entire sink unit — once the norm — are still available, but the join between one of these and the worktop on either side is never so satisfactory. And you lose the uncluttered effect and extra space a long worktop with inset sinks and drainers gives.

Taps of many colours

Taps have become as colourful as sinks. Several firms even co-ordinate them with sinks and hobs. Chrome, of course, is still an option, but now you can have bright red or blue, even white or brass! Taps have changed quite radically, too, on the inside. The ceramic disc, for instance, is now the usual way to regulate the flow of water. The monobloc mixer has made taps with single lever controls possible. These are much more convenient, especially for anyone with arthritic hands.

When choosing taps you need to check how they will relate to the sink(s). Will the tap emerge from the worktop or from the sink surround or even the wall? Spouts should be high enough to allow tall pans and buckets to be filled easily.

Hot rinse taps and detergent dispensers are two of the latest innovations on offer, but the former need a separate water supply.

Waste hole options

Manufacturers offer a range of options to choose from but usually the plumbing under the sink makes one position better than another — or it may even dictate where the waste hole should be.

If you are going to have a waste disposer fitted into a sink, its waste hole must be big enough — the usual diameter is 9 cm/3½ins.

Indispensable or unnecessary?

At the last count under 4% of households in the UK had dishwashers. But the figure is increasing, although there is some way to go before we catch up with the US, where over 40% have a dishwasher. There are many advantages in having one, if you have space and if your budget allows.

• Dishwashers are a much more hygienic way of washing and drying dishes. The water is hotter, the detergent stronger, the drying is done without the aid of human hand or non-sterile tea-towel.

• There is less unsightly clutter, because dirty dishes do not take up valuable sink or drainer space until they are washed up but can be, as it were, filed away in the dishwasher immediately after use.

• They save time, because even if you only use a dishwasher once a day, the loading and unloading will take you at most 15 minutes. Doing the same load by hand would take considerably longer.

• Without the dirty dishes cluttering it up, the sink can be used more intensively as a work centre — as the latest sinks are intended to function, and more compact kitchens demand.

The only disadvantages are that old or fine china with delicate decorations or metallic silver edges should not be washed in a dishwasher — they may be damaged by the detergents and hot water. So only put in crockery and cutlery that is dishwasher proof. Also, you will almost certainly have to wash up some pans and serving dishes by hand after each meal.

Which dishwasher?

Size and cost are usually the determining factors when choosing a dishwasher.

Family dishwashers take between nine and twelve place settings. (A place setting is understood to consist of a soup bowl, a dinner plate, a dessert plate or bowl, a cup and saucer, a glass, a knife and fork, two dessert spoons, a teaspoon and serving dish.)

Of course this is only a rough guide to what a dishwasher holds. You can put whatever you like — or whatever will fit — into the baskets and racks. The average family probably uses its dishwasher once a day during the week, perhaps twice a day at weekends.

Smaller households (one or two people) often feel they do not need so large a dishwasher. One alternative for them is to get a smaller sink-top model which takes two–three place settings. But a family-sized dishwasher with an economy programme (using less water and less electricity) might be a better solution. It could be turned on once a day whether it was full or not and the full programmes would be a great blessing any time extra people were entertained or came to stay.

Costs vary considerably. Many basic models, according to *Which?*, do a very adequate job. They have a choice of programme and, as mechanical parts have been replaced with electronic controls, the six-monthly service visit is a thing of the past.

More expensive models offer more durable construction, noticeably better sound insulation (important if you are usually in the kitchen when it is on) and a larger choice of programmes (an economy programme for instance, or variable spray levels and pressures to cope with the different needs of very delicate glasses or very dirty pans.) The most sophisticated also have micro-chip touch controls.

The smaller table-top models are cheaper than the normal family-sized ones — but there is a much bigger price differential between the standard and the top-price family models.

Whichever dishwasher you choose you will also have to buy special detergent, water softener or salt (in hard water areas) and rinsing agent if you want to get the best results.

Family-sized dishwashers are designed to be plumbed in under a worktop — preferably near the sink and the plumbing, if possible not too far from an outside wall so the waste pipe does not need too long a run. The floor space taken up is the normal unit width of 600mm × 600mm. If your budget can't stretch to a dishwasher straight away, it is worth planning ahead for one by installing its water supply and waste, which would be more expensive to add later.

Many family-size dishwashers can be disguised as part of a run of units, either with a matching decor panel clipped on to the front of the door, or with an integrated matching door that looks exactly like a unit door. Check the possibilities with the manufacturer before you buy.

You should also check up on the service arrangements. Dishwashers don't go wrong so often these days, but the service often varies in speed and efficiency in different parts of the country. Ask people in your area who own dishwashers what their experience of getting service has been.

Right: Two ways of looking at a dishwasher — from the outside and the inside. The luxury version, when closed, matches the units perfectly because it has a matching control panel as well as an integrated door. Its push-button controls are child-proof. The budget version, shown open, has many worth-while features including a two-position upper basket — useful because it can be adjusted to take tall-stemmed glasses when necessary — and adjustable upper spray jets — so you can regulate the water pressure according to the needs of your load.

Whatever style of kitchen you have, this is a perennial problem. Which solution you choose depends on how the rubbish is collected, where the dustbins are, and how much you create. Some alternatives are:

• The small hidden waste bin. A small bin concealed behind unit doors is a discreet solution, to consider only if you don't mind making frequent trips to the dustbin or if you create comparatively little waste.

To avoid the overflowing pedal bin, most units now have room under the sink for a small bin whose lid pops up when you open the unit door. (Woodfit — see page 96 for their address — supply the gadgetry to fit up your own units.) Some manufacturers also offer the alternative of a waste bin in a pull-out fitment as illustrated. In any case, use plastic liners so you can lift the rubbish out without spilling it and seal it hygienically.

• The large, but decorative, dustbin. If you have space for it, bring the dustbin into the kitchen. This has the advantage of cutting down your treks to the dustbins outside. Many dustbins are now plastic, which won't scratch the floor, and decorative, in many cheerful colours besides black.

• Minimising the waste with a waste disposer. It will crunch up most food, vegetable waste, small bones and so on. It only baulks at very fibrous things like corn-on-the-cob centres or artichoke leaves. (One model has optional attachments which can turn the waste disposer into a vegetable peeler, pan scourer or food mixer.) A waste disposer can cut down your rubbish by an estimated 10-15% and another asset is that your dustbin is more hygienic, because everything that rots, smells or attracts vermin will have been disposed of.

On one hand, if taking the rubbish out is an arduous chore — from a flat, or if the bins are some distance away — a waste disposer is invaluable. On the other, if you're a keen gardener and value your compost heap a waste disposer is a waste of money. When choosing a waste disposal unit:

• Choose the best quality you can afford. Check carefully on the servicing and guarantee, as waste disposers have had a reputation for breaking down. (This is why you should only have a waste disposer if you have a second sink.)

• Are waste disposers safe? The "batch-feed" type is as foolproof as you can get — it is loaded when it is off and the grinding only starts when the cover is in position. The continuous feed type is quicker and more convenient because the waste is stuffed down continuously while it is on. It is perfectly safe, providing you follow the loading instructions carefully and the on/off switch is on the wall at the back of the worktop out of small children's reach (as all manufacturers recommend).

• The trash compactor. This reduces dry waste — tins, boards, packaging, etc — to one-quarter of its bulk. At present a trash compactor costs rather more than a dishwasher, so only if you have real problems of waste disposal or collection is it worth investing in one.

Opposite: The dustbin solution in action in a sleek modern kitchen. This one is very large — green to tone in with the pale wood and flourishing plants, plastic so as not to scratch the floor. Rubbish need only be taken out twice a week instead of at least once a day. But a waste-disposer is essential to get rid of food waste and avoid a build-up of unpleasant smells. Also it pays to invest in really tough dustbin liners which don't easily tear.

Right: One of the many ways to hide the waste bin under the sink. Most are pedal-bin size, attached to the door with a clever automatic lid-lifting device. This is one way to fit in a bigger flip-top bin. It is very simply fixed — with an expanding curtain wire or luggage tie.

Match your cooker to your cooking

The questions you ask yourself when considering the general plan of your kitchen become even more relevant when you are choosing your cooker. It is very important that you should work out what kind of cooking you *have* to do everyday and what kind you really *like* doing. The two are not necessarily the same and your cooker needs to satisfy both. For example, continuously-burning stoves, like the Aga or Raeburn, are wonderful if you like baking or making long slow casseroles, while a gas hob gives the best instant control of the heat source — invaluable for sautés as well as fish fingers. A microwave oven demands a whole new approach to cooking which suits some households, but not others! Some specialised appliances are invaluable if you cook with them frequently. Into this category come goodies like those electrically-heated, thermostatically-controlled deep-fryers which can now be set into a worktop. Or turning spits for roasts and kebabs, which are often incorporated into a cooker or oven. If you are particularly keen on barbecue cooking (but not outdoors) an electrically-heated grill which matches the hob unit can give you almost the same effect.

Below. Elegant white hob matches uncluttered units. Points to note: the extra place beside the four hotplates to stand hot pans, the white covers for hotplates not in use, the storage behind the hob for utensils and vital ingredients.

Even when you know quite clearly what kind of cooker suits you, there are still a few more decisions to make.

Size of cooker

It is important to have a big enough cooker, not only to manage the everyday cooking, but also to cope with special occasions: parties, Christmas, weekend guests, visiting children and so on.

A narrow three-ringed cooker which is fine for a small family's daily needs, is a nightmare when you are cooking for 10. Average cookers, hobs and ovens are designed for average families. They do not take kindly to the large casserole, the fish kettle or the preserving pan.

If possible give yourself more flexibility by having too much, rather than too little, cooker area. If a hob is set into the worktop, choose one with a spread-out layout. Or buy Dominos (pairs of rings: see over) and set them a little apart from each other. Or add on an extra pair or a rectangular hotplate in the middle. Freestanding cookers are usually 600mm/24in wide, but you can still get extra wide models. Alternatively, consider a double oven — one large, one small makes for economy and adaptability.

Which fuel do you prefer?

Sometimes your choice is limited by what is available — fuel options for the kitchen as a whole are discussed on pages 30-31.

The type of cooking you do very often dictates the type of fuel you choose. But the choice is complicated today by new options: for example a

Above. White predominates again in this cool kitchen. A white hob is set in its own work area with pan storage below and additional storage at the sides. The white double oven is built-in and consists of a microwave oven at the top and a fan-assisted electric oven with infra red grill below — a combination which copes with most household needs.

Left: Three Domino hob units put together for maximum versatility — a combination vario grill and a two-hotplate hob (both of which can be covered when not in use) plus a ceramic hob. A gas burner could also be incorporated if required.

The other way of treating a freestanding cooker is to put it in its own niche, perhaps a chimney breast, and surround it with pans and utensils needed while cooking.

There is even more choice if you decide on having a separate built-in hob and oven. Hobs come either as one unit — gas or electric burner, or two of each — or you can put together a selection of half-width ones, the so-called Dominos.

Ovens can either be built in under the worktop or fixed at a more convenient height into tall units or directly into a wall. Most of the newest follow the Continental pattern of having the grill at the top of the larger oven but various combinations of single or double ovens or single with microwave are also available.

Ovens and hobs are now made to add colour or complement your decor. As well as the chic browns teamed with smoked glass, there are now primary colours, sludgy earthy colours and fashionable bright white. Whereas colour is a matter of aesthetics, the following are the practical considerations:

Is it easy to clean?

It is worth checking this if you want a clean cooker but don't enjoy removing grime with a caustic cleaner.

Good design affects ease of cleaning to a great extent. Compare old-fashioned gas burners with all their fiddly bits and pieces with the latest sleek gas hobs which have practically no areas where dirt can collect. Ceramic hobs, if you are a careful cook, just need wiping over — the new dark brown or black models show marks much less than the original white ones.

Ovens have become less trouble too. Fan-assisted ovens cook at a lower temperature and so grease splatters do not get burnt on so firmly. Self-cleaning ovens have specially-treated linings from which dirt and grease can be burnt off at high temperatures. Pyrolytic linings are made from specially treated enamel so the dirt incinerates at 500°C when the oven is turned to its special cleaning programme. Catalytic linings dispose of most of the dirt and grease at a mere 300°C and only need to be wiped down afterwards. Ovens that can reach these very high temperatures have to be specially insulated so they are more expensive. A less expensive solution is to have liners which have been treated with a non-stick finish. These make the job of cleaning much easier — but you have to do it regularly.

continuous-burning Aga can now be run on gas or oil as well as solid fuel. Gas ovens have caught up, not only with the automatic timers which only electric ovens once had, but can also be fan-assisted.

Electric ovens are now often described as "multi-functional" which means they can be heated by fan-assisted heat, or normal convection, or both together. Fan-assisted heat has the advantage that as the hot air is circulating all the time, cooking is done at lower temperatures, is more even, and several dishes can be cooked at the same time without transferring tastes.

Ceramic hobs have electric elements, and are slightly slower to cook on than normal electric rings. But the new Haloheat (a British invention) uses tungsten halogen light filaments to produce heat which is as instantly controllable as gas. These hobs also have special ceramic tops.

Microwave cooking needs new techniques altogether but provides new opportunities which are discussed on pages 68–69.

Freestanding or built-in?

This choice depends on the layout of the kitchen and what there is room for.

The latest freestanding cookers are being designed and insulated so they can slot in between units of the standard 600mm/24in module. They look almost as built-in as a built-under oven and hob, but have the advantage that, as they are not technically fixtures, you can take them with you when you move.

Below: The hob line-up that's ready for everything. Matching domino units include two gas rings, two electric hotplates, a full-depth griddle plate, a deep-fat fryer and a heat-resistant parking plate — all inset into the worktop. In the foreground is a useful workmanlike chopping and preparation area. The walls, worktop and units are all easy-to-clean plastic laminate.

Above: Ceramic hob with two Haloheat hotplates and two conventional ones. Haloheat is a revolutionary way of cooking — infra-red light is transmitted through the ceramic hob to the pan. This system gives the lowest possible simmering heat and the fastest heat transmission of any hob. Control is instantaneous which means, for example, that milk which is about to boil over will fall back the moment the plate is switched off.

A kitchen without a cooker seems a contradiction in terms. However, there are now so many cooking appliances available, each with a specialised function, that you could manage to produce meals without a cooker at all, providing you were willing to adapt your menus and your cooking a little to suit the appliances. A selection of appliances, assuming you have room to store them all, could revolutionise cooking in a bed-sit or tiny flat and prove their worth even in a well-equipped kitchen.

Instead of the hob

• Electric kettle. The new tall ones take up less space than the older type and will boil as little as one pint of water at a time, so are more economical. All electric kettles should switch off automatically once they have boiled.

• Electric frying pan/sauté pan/pot roaster/slow cooker. These large, thermostatically-controlled sauté pans with domed lids are extremely versatile — food can either be fried or cooked at a lower temperature for a long time. One model has an earthenware crock as well which turns it into a slow cooker.

• The Slow Cookers. These will cook stews and casseroles at very low temperatures, so if you put them on in the morning, the meal is ready when you come home in the evening. They use no more electricity than a light bulb. Different sizes are available. The cookpot is usually earthenware or Pyrex-type glass.

• The electric deep fryers. These are actually easier to use than a frying pan of fat on top of the stove because of their thermostatic controls.

• There are various other electrically -controlled appliances with specific functions, such as electric coffee machines, electric steamers, electric woks and electric saucemakers.

Instead of the grill

• The infra-red steak grill/sandwich maker/waffle iron. Some of these table-top appliances do one, some (with different cooking plates) do all of these things. Their big disadvantage is while they are in use they create a strong smell and smoke too often, so effective ventilation is needed.

• The pop-up toaster — makes it easier not to burn the toast!

• The rotisserie will grill in the ordinary way or cook chickens and kebabs on a spit and can either be kept on a table top or be built-in.

• The Barbecue. Only a summer alternative, as the smoke and heat cannot easily be dispersed indoors. They come in all sizes and prices from table-top Hibachis to the dome-shaped sputniks on wheels. You can easily build your own outside with a brick framework and metal grids.

Instead of the oven

• Portable oven. Small table-top ovens have been around for some time, but a superior version is a new, small fan-assisted oven, which can be plugged into ordinary 13-amp sockets and easily moved around.

• The Microwave oven. This is almost a replacement for an ordinary oven because you can adapt practically any recipe to microwave techniques. There are problems about browning things (hence the need for special "browning dishes", which you heat up first to sear the meat on, and the appearance of "browning elements") and in cooking items like roast potatoes, Yorkshire pudding and batter recipes, crusty bread, pizzas and meringues. But there are things a microwave does better and faster, like cooking frozen food and anything normally steamed or poached on top of the stove, as well as re-heating meals and keeping them hot. You have to read the manufacturers' instructions carefully and learn how to adapt your recipes. You will also have to adjust your ideas about what to cook in — for example anything metal is not suitable, but some foods can be cooked on paper plates or wrapped in kitchen paper! There are special ranges of containers suitable for microwave ovens, too.

There are already several kinds of microwave ovens to choose from. They can be built-in (to match your wall oven if you like) or table-top. All types can be plugged into a normal 13-amp socket. Some have touch controls, others knobs and dials, many offer two-level cooking, variable power, temperature probes, memory controls and integral grills. Some models distribute the microwaves by rotating the food on a turntable, while others use a stirrer (a kind of fan) to circulate the microwaves round the food. Unfortunately, it has not been decisively shown that one method is better than the other.

Left: Plug-in multi-storey steamer.
Above: Microwave oven — with browning power.
Below: Plug-in all-purpose roasting, frying and casseroling pan.

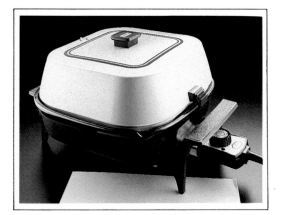

Choosing saucepans and frying pans

The best policy is to get a few of the best quality pans you can afford. On the other hand cheap and cheerful pans will be perfectly all right on gas and are probably a sensible choice when other people besides yourself (lodgers, teenagers) are using your pans as well as you.

The quality of a pan is determined partly by what it is made from and partly by how its base is made. The base is important because it makes contact with the heat source and transfers the heat to the food. Where the heat source is flat (ceramic hob, solid electric ring, Aga) the base must also be flat and heavy in order to heat up evenly and economically. Heavy "ground" bases on pans are designed for this. Thinner bases, suitable for gas or electric radiant rings, will buckle and burn.

Materials commonly used for pans

• Copper. Traditionally the best because it heats up and cools down quickly. Old copper pans need their linings re-tinned regularly, but new ones may have stainless steel linings. The disadvantage is that the copper outside has to be cleaned regularly to keep its coppery shine. In addition, copper pans are always the most expensive.

• Stainless steel. A very practical, long-lasting material for pans — some are guaranteed for 10 years. They're also very easy to keep clean. But as stainless steel is not a good conductor of heat, the bases of these pans must be sandwiched with either aluminium or copper and so the best quality are almost as expensive as copper

• Vitreous enamelled cast iron. This makes good quality pans particularly suitable for cooking over moderate heat or in the oven. They are rather heavy for everyday use, but come in a

good selection of colours. Their price is slightly less than stainless steel.

• Aluminium. Very practical and long-lasting if you choose good quality heavy-gauge aluminium. Today many pans have attractive coloured finishes on the outside and practical non-stick linings inside. They are easy to clean. Medium price for good quality.

• Enamelled steel. These are some of the prettiest pans of all. Some are very cheap and are only suitable for use on gas. Others are tougher, with ground bases. However enamel outside is not so hard-wearing as vitreous enamelled cast iron, and cheaper pans chip easily. Low to medium price, depending on base.

• Toughened glass. Glass has been used for ovenware for a long time, but now there are glass saucepans such as those made by Corning which can be used on top of the stove. Flat-based, easy to clean, inexpensive and not easily broken or chipped.

• Untreated iron and cast-iron. Because iron is an excellent conductor of heat, these are best for frying pans and griddles. If seasoned correctly, they don't rust — the build-up of grease prevents this and acts as a kind of non-stick liner. Keep separate pans for eggs/omelettes, for frying meat and for fish. Inexpensive but heavy.

• Non-stick linings made from polytetra-fluoroethylene (PTFE) are now much longer lasting than they used to be, especially if instructions for initial seasoning and use are followed. Invaluable for milk and scrambled egg pans and also useful on frying pans and bakeware, many aluminium pans and enamelled steel pans of all sizes have these linings. If you like them, buy a set of plastic rather than stainless steel utensils for stirring.

Stainless steel at its very best. Le Pentole pans are a whole new cooking system. Build up into tiers for cooking, stack for storage.

Cast iron in traditional shapes — excellent and economical utensils for frying, grilling and casseroles.

Other points to check when choosing pans

• Handles. A lot of design effort goes into handles but the most important requirement is that they should not get hot — wood or heat-resistant plastic are safest. If you want pans to double as casseroles, choose those with small oven-proof handles on each side.

• Lids must fit well but allow some steam to escape — especially on frying pans. Flat lids which fit several different pans are a practical way of saving storage space.

Dual or triple purpose ovenware

Much ovenware has evolved over centuries to cook one dish perfectly — such as some of the French earthenware casseroles. But today you can save money, storage space and washing up by using dishes which can do two or three things equally well. Some now can go into the oven or microwave (for cooking), on to the table (for serving), into the dishwasher (for cleaning) or the fridge or freezer (for storing) and later on straight back into the oven or microwave. One set will do all this — everything, in fact, except be used on top of the stove. Any dish that does two if not three things is worth having.

A good set of knives

Sharp knives are an essential tool for the cook. Always buy the best quality you can afford, in a variety of sizes.

To keep knives sharp and in good condition store them on a wall magnet, in a knife block or properly fitted drawer. If they are not Lasers (see below) sharpen them regularly.

Knives guaranteed not to need sharpening for 25 years! Laser 5s are made from surgical steel.

Scales

Choose them with both imperial and metric calibrations so you can follow any recipe. The type which can be put back to zero after adding new ingredients are very useful. Scales which fold up to the wall save worktop space. Tops which can be used as mixing bowls are a handy bonus: it's worth buying two, to avoid washing up while cooking.

Stainless steel utensils

No more rusty cheese graters! Stainless steel utensils are well worth the small extra investment because, unlike tin, they will last forever without rusting. But don't use them on pans with non-stick linings — get plastic spatulas and spoons.

Food processors, big mixer or hand beater?

Each of these has its uses and helps the cook in a slightly different way.

If you bake a lot, the big mixer is probably the best choice. Nothing else creams butter and sugar so perfectly or beats up the whites of eggs so high. There are lots of attachments for other jobs, too.

The Food Processor really comes into its own for chopping, slicing, mincing, mixing, puréeing. It saves a lot of hard work for anyone who eats a lot of vegetables, salads and soups. There are attachments for whisking and baking, which are quite adequate if you bake only from time to time. The bigger and stronger your food processor, the better.

Hand beaters are an economical way to mix cakes and beat egg whites more quickly than you could by hand but they can only cope with small quantities at a time, and being smaller and lower-powered, take longer than a big mixer. They are useful for remedial or beating work at the stove — beating up sauces to make them glossy or getting unwanted lumps out of soups!

The Kitchen Machine that does everything — including the work of a mixer, food processor, mincer, blender — Philips versatile space-saver.

First priorities — the fridge and freezer

A refrigerator is the easiest way to organise safe day-to-day storage of perishable foods, while the freezer has revolutionised long-term storage (and, with a microwave, also solves the problem of families whose members all want meals at different times).

Refrigerator temperatures, which are just above freezing (2 — 7°C/35 — 45°F), inhibit the action of the enzymes and bacteria which cause food to deteriorate. Freezer temperatures are lower. They need to be at least −18°C/0°F to store frozen food safely, lower still to freeze it.

What size?

The size you need depends entirely on how you shop (little and often or the large trolleyload once a week), how much food you like to store and the space available in your kitchen.

The most popular size for a fridge is between 5cu ft/141.5 litres and 7cu ft/198 litres. But, as with cookers, a bigger fridge is often invaluable, while too small a one is always inconvenient. If you have no cool store cupboard but room for a big fridge, it is worth getting one with variable temperature zones, so you can keep vegetables, fruit, drinks, etc, at "cellar" temperatures.

Freezers repay thinking big. You can save time and money by bulk purchasing ready-frozen foods, or by freezing your own produce, pickings and made-up dishes. One cubic foot of freezer space will store about 25lb frozen food or freeze 2½lb of fresh food.

Fitting in freestanding models

Because the fridge is an important element in the Work Triangle (pages 18-19) it needs to be positioned conveniently, but with care, so it does not dominate the kitchen visually. The big American food centres or even the taller fridge freezers are better tucked into a recess or

Below: The newest idea for fridges and freezers is easier access with pull-out drawers. The twins here fit under the worktop. Their features include an automatic defrosting and evaporation system and a built-in ventilation system — there are no ducts to spoil the line and as they have fully-integrated doors they match a run of units perfectly. Their capacity is around 3.5 cu ft/100 litres divided between three pull-out shelves.

placed at the end of a row of units. Smaller freestanding models are less difficult to fit in, but instructions about the ventilation necessary must be borne in mind.

Chest freezers take up so much floor space that they are difficult to fit into normal-sized kitchens and are best relegated elsewhere — a Utility Room (see pages 94-95) or even the garage.

Building in

Incorporating the fridge into a run of units avoids having a jarring white expanse (some, but very few, are coloured now) in the middle of the kitchen.

Fridges and freezers can be built into walls or wall units or tucked under worktops. The capacity of the latter type is limited to around 5cu ft/141.5 litres, or less for freezers, which have thicker insulation. Most upright freezers have full-width plastic storage drawers. A few are now being made with pull-out drawers like those in base units, which makes access a little easier.

Right: Here the fridge/freezer is almost completely hidden in a run of elegant wall units because it has integrated doors and matching handles. Any ventilation ducts necessary are concealed in the plinth below.

Below: Traditional family fridge with a freezing compartment is built into a wall of units quite inexpensively because the door has a matching decor panel clipped on to the front.

Built-in fridge freezers are limited in size only by the need to match in with the units and so are nearly always within the 600mm module. You can have twins side by side or different sizes, one above the other. If the freezer is in the lower position you avoid bending so much. Doors can be matched to units either by clipping a decor panel over the fronts, or by attaching a unit door to the fridge door so they both open together — these integrated doors are the best match.

Other options

Differences between manufacturers are generally details of styling, door handles, interior fittings, ingenious use of door storage, extra gadgets like ice-makers and water coolers, right or left-hand opening doors. A worthwhile extra on expensive models is automatic defrosting.

Running costs

Running costs on electricity are estimated to amount to the price of one unit per day for refrigerators, one to two units per cubic foot per week for freezers. There are a few refrigerators, including one fridge-freezer, that will run on gas or calor gas; these have the advantage of running silently!

Do you need a larder as well as a refrigerator? Most people with both find they would not like to part with either! A good old-fashioned larder has many virtues which complement those of a refrigerator.

The conditions provided by a traditional larder are ideal for storing certain foods and drink. The temperature (between 8 and 15°C/47 and 59°F), the currents of cool air, the slight humidity, all combine to create the right ambience for keeping many vegetables at their best. Fruit ripens slowly. Hams, cheeses and game mature naturally, so will wines, beer and cider. Jams, preserves and freshly-dried herbs like the darker corners. Left-overs don't have all their taste chilled out of them.

Traditional larders were built to tried and tested specifications: sited on the north side of the house, they had thick walls and the materials used were chosen because they were slow to warm up — hence the stone or brick floors, the slate or marble shelves. Air-bricks, or sometimes small windows, created cooling air currents.

If your house has a larder like this, it is an asset to cherish. For modern houses and flats other alternatives have to be explored. Luckily new ideas are emerging.

Some big refrigerators now have several different temperature zones, one of which provides a cellar temperature between 5 and 15°C. (Big American fridges have been offering this for some time — at a price). There are now several "Larder" fridges to choose from: 9cu ft or more, sometimes without freezing compartments, but with one area for chilling and another, less cold, for storing "larder products", each with its own thermostat.

A new luxury idea is the ventilated store cupboard. This has an air circulating unit which can also cool the air, especially if the cupboard is placed against an outside wall. It won't chill food but is excellent for dry stores, vegetables, jams, herbs and wine.

Wire mesh drawers in a unit are a simple, comparatively economical compromise. The mesh allows air to circulate within the unit. If possible an air brick through to an outside wall will give extra ventilation.

Left: The traditional larder in all its glory — the invaluable ally of a productive gardener and wine-maker.
Right: A sophisticated ventilated store-cupboard which matches other Bulthaup units.

The store cupboard

Temperatures are not critical for most non-perishable supplies normally kept on kitchen shelves or in the store cupboard.

Today, you are helped by the "Best Before" date which many goods now display. This is designed to help you, the buyer, when shopping, but it is also invaluable for stock control at home. Modern packaging keeps things in good condition up to the "Best Before" date, provided your kitchen is not too humid, too light (for some things) or infested with pests (like mice).

Keeping things dry

In a kitchen which has adequate heating and ventilation there is little danger, in this country, of the humidity being too high. The problem more often arises in second houses which are not visited regularly in winter.

Damp ruins dry goods — flour, tea, spices, biscuits, packet soups and so on. Jams and preserves will go mouldy. Tinned foods (all of which keep for at least a year and often much longer under normal conditions) are in danger because if the tin gets rusty, pinpoint holes in the metal can appear, air can get in and the contents ruined.

As an indicator, if salt in its packet is clogging, conditions are too damp to store anything for long. You can, of course, transfer any goods to airtight containers but few of the pretty tins and jars sold for this purpose really are airtight; only jars with rubber seals and tins and plastic containers that specifically claim to be airtight can be relied on.

If you don't have good ventilation and/or your kettle boiling or vegetables cooking create a lot of steam, keep your long-term stores away from the vapour, either in a closed cupboard or another room.

Some stores need darkness

Herbs and spices lose their colour and flavour if kept in daylight. They are best stored away from the light, but even so, dried herbs lose flavour by the end of 12 months. Jams and preserves also keep better inside a cupboard than on open shelves.

Discouraging pests

The advantage of refrigerators, freezers and well-made modern units with backs as opposed to shelves and cupboards or units without backs, is that the former keep their contents protected against insect pests, mice and household pets, all of which will contaminate food. Flies spread bacteria everywhere and lay their eggs on meat products. Other insects go for cereals and farinaceous stores. Mice seem to eat everything (including plastic!) Your dogs and cats are not only born thieves, given half a chance, but can also contaminate food.

Stock control

No amount of packaging or even temperature and humidity control will protect goods for ever. Your contribution must be methodical stock control. Make sure you use your stores before they start to deteriorate!

Even canned goods have a restricted shelf life. For example, canned milk products, prunes and rhubarb only last up to 12 months. Most other canned foods should be used within 18 months to two years. Only solid-pack cold meat products and fish in oil keep for as long as five years.

Flour, even in airtight containers, has a surprisingly short life. Plain flour should be used within six months, self-raising within three months and wholemeal can go off within two months.

Below: A store cupboard that's roomy and pest-proof, and matches other units.

Above: We've shown other views of this kitchen because it is so full of good storage ideas — see pages 50-51. The Shaws designed this handsome — if not very extensive — wine rack to match in with the rest of their kitchen. (They have restricted themselves to under three dozen bottles.) They have carefully positioned it away from heat sources and vibrating machines in a place where only their light-footed cats tread frequently.

The wine cellar

Bringing fine wines to maturity needs special expertise and precise control of temperature and humidity not possible in most households. Keeping wine a few weeks before you drink it is another matter. According to experts at the Wine Society, "Wine is best stored horizontally in a dark place which is insulated as far as possible from temperature changes and ventilation." Hence the popularity of the cellar for keeping wine.

But it is quite satisfactory to have a wine rack in a dark corner of the kitchen or utility room where the temperature is more or less constant and does not go over 70°F. Keep it away from the washing machine and any other heat source. Laying bottles on their side is advisable to ensure that the cork keeps moist. If it dries out, air can get in and spoil the wine, which is then said to be "corked". This is a rare occurrence if you can't manage to keep your bottles unopened for long.

Left: The wine rack under this island unit is one of the classic types: the bottles lie on their sides, cradled on metal supports. Other popular and readily-available racks have diamond-shaped or square-shaped frameworks and can be put together, in units of dozens, to fit snugly into most spaces. A full wine rack always looks decorative so it is a pity to hide your bottles behind unit doors.

Above: One dominating colour is the dramatic starting point for the decorative scheme in this kitchen. Tones of cerulean blue contrast with white tiling up the walls and link the separate visual elements in the room, such as the idiosyncratic cooker, the two tables and all the kitchen paraphernalia on display. What this kitchen lacks in terms of work-flow convenience it makes up for in charm!

The backbones of a colour scheme

When you have worked out what sort and style of kitchen you want and planned where the units are to go and which appliances you need you are ready to think about decorating and working out colour schemes.

This is the stage when you start to give your well-planned kitchen its own individual identity, different from every other well-planned kitchen.

How to start building up a colour scheme

First find some peg to start your imagination working. For instance, you may just like certain colours in a kitchen: the whites and blue-greys which look so cool and fresh, or warm and welcoming splashes of bright primary colour. You may already have something which could inspire a colour scheme — such as a red Aga, some tiles you specially like, a collection of china or a picture. The units you choose will, of course, affect what colours you have elsewhere.

Sometimes the style of a kitchen demands certain colours. For instance, the recognizable colours for High Tech kitchens are black, white and grey (including aluminium and chrome finishes) with, possibly, a primary colour. Many kitchens in the Sixties and Seventies hardly bothered with colour as such but relied on the juxtaposition of natural materials (wood, brick, flagstones, etc) for the overall effect.

Rooms themselves often suggest certain colours. If they are small, it is worth bearing in mind that lighter colours will make them look

larger and that one colour can unify a lot of odd shapes into a whole.

If the kitchen is part of, or leads off, the living or dining room, the colours in that room must influence what you choose for the kitchen.

Collecting the samples

Your next step is to translate your ideas into particular floor coverings, wall colours, tiles and accessories, as well as co-ordinating your worktops, cooker, sink, taps and units.

This involves a lot of research into what's available, juggling with your ideas and ingenuity when what you really want is not available or much too expensive. But eventually things begin to fall into place and you can start, like a professional designer, making up a sample board. You can fake the artist's impression designers create for their clients by finding photos of your units, floor coverings, wall colours,

Above: A clever juxtaposition of different materials is the basis of this Scandinavian scheme. White walls, natural wood shelves and drawers, wood-trimmed white units, white chrome and metal chairs are all set off by the unusual ceramic floor which is predominantly white but spiked with tiles of different primary colours. Its pattern is repeated on a smaller scale on the blinds.

etc. This will help you get an over-all picture of how your ideas might look in practice.

The practical side

Three important elements have a major impact on every kitchen decoration scheme: the floor, the walls and ceiling and the lighting. These all interact with each other, of course, but each one has also to be chosen with certain practical functions in mind which are just as important as getting the colour and style right.

The kitchen floor gets the hardest, most intensive wear of any room in a house. So, above all other considerations, the floor covering you choose must be able to stand up to this. It must also be easy to keep clean and hygienic, and be unaffected by spills of grease, food, acids or liquids.

All the materials discussed below are practical in these ways. Some cost a lot more than others, some need laying by a professional. Prices are simplified here into categories of Low, Medium, High and Luxury to give you an idea of relative costs. Prices do of course vary from shop to shop and year to year and they also depend a lot on whether you can lay the floor yourself or need to have a professional do it for you.

It is worth investing in a good floor if you think you will be in the house long enough to get the benefit of its quality, or if you calculate that a high quality floor in a luxury kitchen will add to the price of the house when you sell. If you can only look ahead a couple of years, and would not get your money spent on the floor back, you will probably find the low-price solutions (vinyl, stripped boards or carpet tiles) adequate.

Some floors are easier to maintain than others. For example, cork or wood with a polyurethane seal needs new coats of seal before the old one wears through, sometimes as often as every 12 months. Vinyl or vinyl-topped coverings, on the other hand, should need no further maintenance.

The sub-floor

It is vital to prepare this properly if any floor covering is to wear well. The sub-floor must be level, free from, and, preferably, stripped, of all previous floor coverings.

A concrete or solid floor at ground level should have a damp-proof membrane so it is dry. Unless it is in very good condition it will also probably need a top latex screed (or an alternative proprietary treatment) to make it smooth and level. Various self-levelling screeds are available which are not too difficult for the amateur to apply. Any covering can be laid on this surface.

A timber or sprung floor first needs to have all its floorboards firmly fixed and all the nails punched down. Then hardboard or plywood is laid over the boards and tacked down every 10cm/4in. Most floor coverings can be laid over this, but ceramic tiles need additional preparation to prevent movement. It is best to get professional advice about this.

Wood — stripped floorboards

This is the cheapest way to deal with the floor if you prepare, sand and seal the floorboards yourself! They can afterwards be painted, stencilled or stained, and sealed again for protection.

Maintenance: keep coats of seal in good condition.
Cleaning: wash with minimum water on a sponge mop.
Laying: DIY
Price: low.

Vinyl sheet

Now available in a very wide choice of colours and textures, including convincing look-alikes for tiles, cork, wood and even studded rubber. Cushion backing makes it a warm, comfortable and very practical floor covering.
Maintenance: none. Some vinyl sheet is guaranteed for five years, but can melt under intense heat such as a burning cigarette or very hot oven shelf.
Cleaning: very easy; use water on a sponge mop.
Laying: DIY. Many makes come in widths up to 4m/13ft and can be loose laid without sticking down.
Price: low.

Vinyl tiles (thin)

As vinyl sheet but less choice of patterns and no cushion backings.
Laying: DIY. Some brands come with self-stick backings, but all must be stuck down.
Price: low.

Thick vinyl tiles

These are of a different quality from ordinary vinyl, being thicker, harder and much longer wearing — in fact they come into the "last a lifetime" category. In addition they are made in an exceptionally good range of colours, textures and patterns and so give a high quality feel to a kitchen.
Maintenance: none.
Cleaning: vacuum or sweep; wash occasionally with minimum water on a sponge mop. Highly textured patterns are recommended for kitchens as they show marks less than plain ones.
Laying: professional laying recommended, but could be done by skilled DIY.
Price: high.

Carpet tiles

If you like the idea of a carpet in a kitchen, the newest polypropylene carpet tiles are very different from the original rough hairy squares. They have a tight finish like a fine Berber twist and come in discreet and subtle shades.
Maintenance: none; some guaranteed five years.
Cleaning: vacuum. Spills can be mopped up with a cloth. Single tiles can be scrubbed or even replaced if disaster strikes.
Laying: DIY. No need to stick down.
Price: low.

Opposite: A grand, almost Palladian, effect of terrazzo mosaic inlaid with marble strips — actually achieved with thick vinyl tiles laid imaginatively. This floor should last a lifetime.

Cork

Cork tiles have a natural look and are warm, resilient and comfortable underfoot. They are a favourite choice for family kitchens.
Maintenance: cork must be very well sealed and kept in good condition by frequent re-sealing in areas of heavy use, otherwise the cork discolours and turns grey.
Cleaning: wash with minimum water on a sponge mop.
Laying: DIY. Stick down with recommended adhesive and add final coat(s) of seal afterwards.
Price: low.

Vinyl-topped cork

These cork tiles are actually a thin layer of cork between layers of vinyl, the top layer being transparent, combining the advantages of cork with the easy-care qualities of vinyl. Available in rectangular shapes as well as square, some brands with different cork effects.
Maintenance: none.
Cleaning: vacuum; wash with mimimum water on a sponge mop.
Laying: sub-floor must be level and damp-proof. DIY for the competent.
Price: medium

Nylon carpet (Flotex)

A unique floor covering: hardwearing, practical enough for garages and factories as well as kitchens in the home. Resembling very close-cropped carpet, it's dense (40,000 fibres to the square inch!) and bonded to a waterproof vinyl base. Unfortunately the available designs are not yet in the same class as its performance.
Maintenance: none; guaranteed for 21 years. Cigarettes can burn it and corrosive cleaners damage it if not cleaned off immediately.
Cleaning: vacuum. Spills can be mopped off surface.
Laying: DIY. No underlay needed. Secure edges with double-edged tape.
Price: medium.

Lino

This is still available, though largely superseded by the cheaper, more practical vinyls. Usually available in very subtle marbled colours.
Maintenance: feed regularly with non-slip polish to keep it supple. If sealed, re-seal at regular intervals.
Cleaning: wash with minimum water on a sponge mop.
Laying: DIY, but needs to be stuck down. Big sheets which have to be joined at the seams need heat-sealing by a professional.
Price: medium.

Rubber

Rubber is currently enjoying a revival in the form of the Pirelli studded rubber effect copied from offices and warehouses by high-tech designers. Flooring suitable for domestic uses (2.7mm/⅛in thick) is actually made from synthetic rubber: rubber itself is unnecessarily hard-wearing and too expensive for home use. There is now a choice of very good colours as well as black.
Maintenance: none.
Cleaning: vacuum and, if necessary, wipe off stains with damp cloth. Can be polished occasionally with wax emulsion in a water solution.
Laying: professional laying recommended.
Price: high.

Vinyl-topped wood

Made on the same principle as vinyl-topped cork, these planks have a wood veneer between layers of cork and vinyl. The impression, when laid, is of a natural wood floor.
Maintenance: none.
Cleaning: vacuum; wash with sponge mop.
Laying: professional laying recommended but could be done by very skilled DIY.
Price: high.

Ceramic tiles

There is a very wide choice of beautiful tiles. Bear in mind that tiles suitable for floors are heavier and more expensive than wall tiles and different from worktop tiles. Like all hard floors they are hard on the feet and anything that is dropped on them tends to break. On the plus side, they add quality to a kitchen and wear for ever.
Maintenance: nothing, except to check that the grouting is kept in good condition.
Cleaning: wash with a damp sponge mop.
Laying: sub-floor needs special preparation and professional laying is recommended.
Price: high to very high depending on the tiles chosen.

Quarry tiles

Earthy colours and bricky textures make quarry tiles particularly sympathetic to country-style kitchens. They have the same disadvantages as ceramic tiles.
Maintenance: none.
Cleaning: as ceramic tiles above.
Laying: the weight of quarry tiles makes them unsuitable for laying on timber sub-floors. Professional laying recommended.
Price: high.

Marble

Although Mediterranean kitchens have marble floors, in Britain they are rare. Marble is expensive, and can stain; its main attribute (apart from its beauty) is its coolness — a quality not particularly prized or needed in chilly climates.
Maintenance: none
Cleaning: simple unless acidic liquids spill; wash with damp sponge mop.
Laying: must be professionally laid on a solid sub-floor.
Price: very high.

Above: A strong natural floor to complement not only the simple wood furnishings but also the view out of the window. But the 3-D ceramic tile effect is an illusion: it is the design on thick linoleum tiles, which are almost as long-lasting as the real thing!

Terrazzo

This is created out of marble chippings embedded in a special cement. It is so handsome and practical that nearly every fashionable Italian restaurant in London has a terrazzo floor. However it is also expensive!
Maintenance: none.
Cleaning: wash with damp sponge mop. Does not stain.
Laying: terrazzo is created on the floor as it is laid and then polished and finished. So it has to be laid professionally on a specially prepared solid sub-floor.
Price: very high.

Slate

Wales's answer to marble, now nice enough to grace the most expensive "simple" country kitchens! Handsome and practical too. (See a worktop made of slate on page 57).
Maintenance: none.
Cleaning: wash with damp sponge mop.
Laying: professional laying on a very good solid sub-floor.
Price: very high.

Flagstones, brick, etc.

It is a wonderful bonus to have one of these old floors in your kitchen, even if it is in less than perfect condition, because it contributes such character and quality to the room. Plan the units and decor to harmonise with it.
Maintenance: none.
Cleaning: unless you seal them with polyurethane varnish, these floors tend to give off dust. When sealed they can be swept or washed.
Laying: it is rarely possible to get used ones today, but if you need originals ask a good builder.
Price: they just come with the house – or not!

The colours and textures of wall coverings make a large contribution to the look of a kitchen. In fact, changing them is often the quickest and cheapest way to give the whole kitchen a new look. In practical terms only the walls behind the worktop and around the sink and cooker really have to be waterproof and easily wipeable. This is why tiles are often chosen for this part of the wall, while the rest of the kitchen is painted or papered.

As with floors, however, the condition of the walls and ceiling you are going to decorate is important — they must be properly prepared before painting or papering. Although you can paper or paint over any surface which has been cleaned and primed, if the wall is first stripped of its old paint or paper the result will look more professional and last longer.

Paint

Paint gives you the widest possible colour choice, and, in addition, you can also paint on textures or get original effects by dragging, rag-rolling, spongeing or stencilling.

Traditionalists insist on an oil-based paint in a gloss or eggshell finish for kitchen walls, but emulsion paint with a silk finish also gives a slightly glossy look and can be wiped clean. Gloss is still hardest-wearing for woodwork, but any oil-based paint is also suitable.

Price: low — especially DIY.

Wallpapers

Vinyl-coated papers are specially made for kitchens and bathrooms, but any paper which can be sealed with a protective coat of thinned polyurethane or a proprietary wallpaper sealer without the colours running, is suitable anywhere, except behind the worktop, sink or cooker.

Price: depends entirely on paper chosen. DIY.

Below: Unusual treatment for a window wall above the worktop — grey painted panelling with white surround has a stencilled grey floral border.

Above: Wall of tiles creates another window and another view! Trompe l'oeil *view is painted on tiles before glazing and fitted together on site.*

Ceramic tiles and mosaics

A wonderful choice of colours, sizes, designs and price and a very practical solution for the walls behind the worktop and sink and around the cooker.

Tiles of any sort must be fixed to walls in good condition. Epoxy grout is more difficult to apply than the normal kind, but is much more hard-wearing and waterproof. Grout can be tinted to match or contrast with tiles.

Price: medium if you choose standard tiles, or mosaic sheets and DIY. High, if you choose expensive or irregular tiles and have them fixed to large areas of the wall by a professional.

Panelling

Wood panelling is most often tongued and grooved pine, but any seasoned wood can be used. Some unit manufacturers will also provide panelling in solid wood to match their unit doors.

It is also possible to get plastic laminate panelling (including wood-grain look-alikes) for walls; this has unlimited possibilities for colour and design.

Providing that the panelling has a wipe-down finish, it is a good way to disguise walls in poor condition. But all panelling has to be fixed to a framework of battens which makes it a DIY job only for the skilful handy person.

Price: medium to high depending on the panelling chosen (and higher if put up professionally!)

It is a great advantage to have good natural light in a kitchen. It gives you endless variety, because the quality of light changes with the hours, the days, and the seasons.

Good windows in a kitchen are a bonus. Unusual ones give it character. Kitchens fitted with large expanses of glass, like a conservatory, are irresistible.

Unless there are strong reasons for obscuring the view from the windows, it pays to think of window treatments in terms of letting in as much light as possible during the day.

At night, for the reverse effect, you need curtains or blinds or shutters which can be drawn, pulled or shut easily.

Only if you want to shut out neighbours, passers-by or an extremely depressing view twenty-four hours a day should you think of forgoing what natural light there is altogether.

Whatever window treatment you decide on, make sure it is easy to keep clean. Even with really good ventilation, the atmosphere in a kitchen contains more odours, water vapour, smoke and grease than in any other room. So curtains should be washable, blinds spongeable. In addition any blind or curtain which is anywhere near a cooker ought to be flame-proofed to cut down the risk of fire; in fact, flapping curtains near a heat source are best avoided altogether.

Apart from these considerations, the choice of window treatments suitable for kitchens is as varied as for any other window in the house. Some practical alternatives are:

Roller Blinds

Roller blinds are increasingly popular, especially for windows above a sink or worktop, because they take up so little room and can be pulled up or down without disturbing all things that, inevitably, live on the window sill or worktop. There's a very wide choice of plain colours, patterns and original designs. As most fabrics can be stiffened to make them suitable for blinds, blinds can match up with curtains, cushions, tablecloths, etc, elsewhere.

Prices range from cheap DIY kits to specially designed originals whose price depends on who designed them.

Variations on roller blinds

Roller blinds made from split cane, fine wood or plastic slats, pinoleum and so on give a slightly different effect. By day, if rolled down, the light

Three different effects with blinds. Shadowed light, blurred view, soft texture is the effect of natural pinoleum (top). A fresh, contemporary look comes from this clean, crisp roller blind (centre). Venetian blind (below) has natural wood slats to reflect light, echo wood worktop.

filters through them interestingly. By night you can see out — but passers-by can see in.

Roman blinds

Roman blinds, instead of rolling up on a roller, fold themselves up in a series of big pleats. Any fabric is suitable as long as it is washable; even so, in a kitchen they are not very easy to keep clean — although infinitely preferable to festoon blinds in this respect.

Venetian blinds

These are a good-looking solution for all types of kitchen except the one which aims for a traditional country atmosphere.

They are now available in narrow slats as well as wide ones and made in wood, too. There are lots of colours and even a mirror finish to choose from.

Dust frequently, otherwise cleaning eventually becomes a terrible chore.

Vertical louvre blinds

These are the best answer if you like louvre effects but don't want to dust frequently.

They are made from strips of stiffened fabric with a track at the top of the window and various patented ways of adjusting their opening angle. There's quite a choice of colours and patterns or you can opt for a dramatic picture painted over the whole set of louvres.

Café curtains

If you must have curtains, café curtains are a good solution when the window is over the sink or worktop. At the correct height (just above eye level) they stop people looking in, but allow daylight to come in above. Because they generally remain drawn the whole time, they never need disturb the plants and objects which have gathered in front of them.

Shutters

Traditional shutters which fold in beside the window need a certain amount of free space around them for opening and shutting. Where space is limited, or traditional shutters unsuitable, a good solution could be fixed shutters with inset adjustable louvre panels which can be opened and shut without moving the shutters themselves.

These shutters can be fixed, like café curtains, to cover either the lower half of the window, or, in the manner of American Deep South interiors, the whole area.

Some ideas for blocking off a poor outlook

There are a number of alternatives to frosted glass. For instance, if the window gets enough light for plants to flourish, fix a set of shelves in front of it. Crowded with plants and herbs this makes an effective screen.

Even with poor light, you can make an effect with dried flowers, pottery and plates and so on. Obviously you need to arrange alternative ventilation so the window can always remain closed.

A more radical solution is to screen off the window altogether. You can use strong paper, fabric, pierced hardboard — each of these with an additional light behind it can give an interesting effect. Plain hardboard would provide a base on which to stick a poster or paint a *trompe l'oeil* view.

Left: Burgeoning greenery in the window box outside, kitchen pots and pans and more plants on shelves across the window inside — all add up to a lively substitute for curtains, blinds or shutters and give life to a drab outlook.

There are two separate kinds of lighting to plan for in a kitchen: natural light and artificial light. Each affects the decoration scheme differently.

Natural light

Good daylight is an asset in any kitchen, as the previous pages have shown. A bright, sunny room is a pleasant place to work in, so if you are planning a kitchen from scratch and have a choice of rooms to put it in, you should obviously think about the quality of natural light the room will have. Would sunlight in the morning or afternoon be more useful to you? Will a south-facing room be too hot in summer, a north-facing one too dark in winter?

If the site of the kitchen is fixed, perhaps minor structural changes, such as enlarging an existing

Above: High-tech lighting spills light efficiently over a central worktop. As they are designed for industrial use, the fittings are heavy and have to be supported by special wire. The flexes, which don't take any weight, are looped up casually, in keeping with the high-tech atmosphere.

window or putting in a new one, could increase the natural light available (see pages 26-27).

Lights to turn on the atmosphere

Artificial lighting for kitchens has been transformed. The harsh fluorescent tube across the ceiling is now a thing of the past.

Lighting now makes a positive contribution to kitchen decor. First, the choice of fittings — from copies of Victorian billiard table lights to clamp-on industrial spotlights — sets the style.

Above:For task lighting over the worktop these bulbs, with wire protectors rather than shades, have been fixed below eye level to avoid glare. General lighting comes from an up-lighter (concealed behind plant) and ceiling lamps with outsize bulbs.

Left: This kitchen has a very specific lighting blueprint. A window on the right-hand wall (not shown here) brings general daylight into the room. But the hob and the island worktop need their own specific lighting by day as well as night. So the hob niche has been provided with its own fluorescent lights, concealed behind a baffle to cut down glare. The island worktop is very effectively lit up by two ceiling downlighters positioned above it which also contribute to the general light level of the kitchen after dark.

Second and more important, perhaps, is the way lighting changes the atmosphere by enabling you to light — brightly, dimly or not at all — separate areas of the kitchen in different ways. This is especially valuable if you eat in the kitchen and want a more relaxed kind of lighting to eat by than to work by.

You can divide up the lighting in the kitchen according to what you need at different times. Sometimes you will need a working light, sometimes a general light, sometimes a spotlight, sometimes a light to eat by. If you put each type of lighting on its own switch and, except for the working lights, put each switch on a dimmer, you will achieve a very flexible lighting scheme. You will be able to have bright lighting in one area, dim lighting in another. You will be able to create a party atmosphere as easily as a very business-like one.

Lights to work by

It is most important to have good task lights over the worktop, the sink and the cooker — over any working area in fact. If there are wall units or wide shelves over the worktop, small fluorescent tubes can be fixed under them behind a batten which matches or co-ordinates with the units or shelves. These are ideal because they throw a shadowless light down on the worktop.

If you have an up-to-date cooker hood with an extractor fan, it will also have its own built-in light which comes on when you open the hood.

If there are no cupboards over the work surface, the best lighting solution would be to install a row of downlighters placed in line over the middle of the worktop. These give a good light without glare. The shade, a long cylinder, can either be recessed up into the ceiling, partly recessed or not recessed at all, depending on how much space there is between the kitchen ceiling and the floor above.

General lighting

How much general light you need depends on how large the kitchen is, whether you also have special objects or pictures you want to accentuate , and what style of lighting suits your kitchen. You also have to be able to see into cupboards and drawers, although ovens and refrigerators now have their own lights.

Downlighters make good general lights as well as working lights, when fixed into the ceiling at intervals.

Spotlights are another possibility. They can either be mounted on a track, semi-recessed into a ceiling or set on a wall. Their light is most effective when bounced off a wall or the ceiling rather than directed straight at a worktop or table; then they are less likely to catch your eye and glare as you move about.

If you don't want to go to the expense of having specially fitted lights and already have a central ceiling rose, big round white Japanese paper shades (cheap to buy and cheap to replace) give

Above: Effective night lighting in a no-nonsense kitchen. General light is provided by downlighters in the ceiling. Concealed strip-lights give shadowless illumination to the worktop, hob and sink. Decorative light comes from ceiling washers hidden on top of the units.

a pleasant general light, as more than one poverty-stricken but design-conscious home-owner has found! Even an ornamental umbrella hung upside down deflects the central light nicely.

Lights to eat by

If there is a table in the kitchen, the rise and fall fitting (with whatever shade suits your kitchen) is invaluable. You can adjust it so it just lights the table while you eat, and raise it when you want a general light or have to move the table. If it has its own dimmer switch it is even more versatile.

Clockwork rise and fall mechanisms (within a curly flex) have a limited adjustment of about 60cm/2ft. This is enough for average height ceilings, but for a bigger differential, you will need a more elaborate mechanism with weights.

The trend to informal mealtimes

Some occasions are dining-room occasions and some people are dining-room people. But both are on the decline, with the result that more and more meals, snacks and even dinner parties are taking place around the kitchen table.

There are many advantages to eating in the kitchen. It fits in with life with young children, with teenagers who grab their food and run, with busy working couples and with older people cutting down on unnecessary work.

It also fits in with our increasingly informal lifestyles. For many families in Britain, Sunday lunch is the only old-style family meal of the week. People who think of entertaining as a way to relax rather than putting on a show very often choose to dine in their kitchen.

Family Kitchens (see pages 12-13) have always allowed for sit-down meals. In Unkitcheny Kitchens (see pages 10-11) the very nature of the open plan arrangement means that the table is adjacent to where the food is cooked as well as the sofa where you sit and have coffee afterwards. Even in compact Workshop Kitchens (see pages 14-15), ways can often be found to incorporate somewhere to sit and eat.

Below. Kitchen table prepared for a sit-down meal — the informal folding chairs can be stored away neatly when not needed.

How much space to allow

For comfort, each person needs a place at least 60cm/2ft wide and 38cm/15ins deep. The depth allowed would of course depend on the style of the chair — a ladder-back or director's chair for instance, would be space savers; while a bentwood chair or anything with an outward curve would obviously take more room.

You can provide for sit-down meals which take up less space by having the table in a corner and fixed bench seating. Snacks and informal meals need even less space if you take them at a bar or worktop and either stand or keep stools under it.

In a small kitchen, you can create extra space by having a table top that pulls out from the units when you need it. This would just be big enough (coming out of a 600mm/24in unit) for two people to eat at, or three to drink a cup of coffee or tea round. In this case you need somewhere to stow away stools or chairs: fold-up chairs can be hung up on the back of a door, for instance.

Where to place the table

It is best to think of the kitchen as two areas which may overlap: a working area and an eating area.

Even where there is room for a big pine table in the kitchen, try to place it so that it does not interfere with the work triangle and interrupt movement between the cooker, sink and refrigerator/food stores.

Some division between the work area and the eating area is advantageous because you are distanced from the dirty pans in the sink during your meal. This division can be created with a peninsular or island unit without losing the informality of eating in the kitchen. At night the lighting can be arranged so that the table is illuminated while you eat and the working lights over the sink turned off — see the lighting discussed on pages 88-91.

Style of tables and chairs

A popular solution is to use very kitcheny chairs and table — old chopped-on pine for the table, stick-back or ladder-back country chairs and milking stools-anything, in fact, redolent of traditional farmhouse kitchens.

But you have to think again when the design of the kitchen is in a different style. A number of continental manufacturers, as well as making kitchen units, also design tables, chairs and wall storage to match. This could be a good solution for an unkitcheny or workshop kitchen. But there are many other alternatives: remember to keep within the style of your kitchen and avoid anything too formal, too difficult to clean or too demanding.

It is not too difficult to ring the changes in the atmosphere you create - even though the table is in the kitchen - if you exploit different lighting possibilities and if you lay the table imaginatively. For children's breakfast plastic animal mats, simple china or unbreakable melamine are just right. The same table can be transformed in the evening with a tablecloth, napkins, bone china, sparkling glass and different lighting.

Below. Dining area here has formal chairs which emphasise its separation from the pots and pans.

Invaluable extra space

One way to make your kitchen a pleasanter place in which to work is to remove as much as possible that is not directly concerned with preparing, cooking and eating food altogether, and create a well-planned utility room.

It is a comparatively new idea to spend money specially fitting up a utility room: usually people just install old or second-hand storage, a utilitarian worktop and a sink that was already in the house. But having a well-planned utility room does make a lot of household chores pleasanter and can even reduce the skivvying aspect of housework. For these reasons, such an area is becoming an important consideration when people are looking for a house.

Fitting up a utility room does not necessarily mean buying a second lot of expensive units. But the same criteria that make a kitchen work well also apply to a utility room. Floor, wall and worktop surfaces must be practical and hard-wearing, as it is an even more functional room than the kitchen. But on the other hand, it also benefits from a pleasant colour scheme, from being easy to keep clean, and even from having carefully chosen lighting rather than an all-purpose fluorescent strip glaring down.

What can go into a Utility Room?

The Boiler

This is an obvious candidate since it is not strictly necessary in the kitchen, unless it is a continuous burning one designed to heat the room. Modern boilers need servicing once or twice a year and this is more convenient if the boiler is outside the kitchen.

Laundry equipment

The kitchen is not the best place for washing and drying clothes. Dirty washing is unhygienic near food and clean or drying clothes pick up cooking smells all too easily. In an ideal labour-saving utility room there would be a sink for soaking and handwashing, an automatic washing-machine either with its own drying cycle or a twin tumble dryer, and a drying rack for delicate fabrics, or for when it is impractical to hang things outdoors. Ironing could also be done there, in which case storage is needed for the ironing-board and iron as well as for detergents, dirty clothes and clothes to be ironed or aired or mended.

Cleaning equipment

Brooms, mops, dustpans, vacuum cleaners, their accessories and bags, not to mention the whole range of detergents and cleaning materials every household amasses are all ideally kept in a utility room.

China, glass, etc

All the china and glass which is not in everyday use, especially if there is no separate dining room, can go into a china cupboard together with extra serving dishes, large pans, flower vases and so on. Glass doors are a good idea because they are transparent, but keep off the dust. Any doors are better than none!

Extra food storage

This is the best place for a chest freezer if you have a lot of garden produce to freeze, cook professionally or live a long way from the shops. Chest freezers are difficult to fit into normal kitchens, but are the most economical way of getting a lot of freezer space. If there is a pest-proof cupboard, you can save store cupboard space in the kitchen by keeping your reserve and/or bulk-bought stores here too.

Wine cellar

In a house with no cellar, the Utility Room is often a good place to store wine, as long as the boiler does not make it too warm, and the washing machine and dryer do not cause vibrations.

Pets

Anything to do with pets — food, plates, beds, grooming equipment, and litter — is best kept out of the kitchen for reasons of hygiene.

Alternatives to a utility room

If there is simply no space for a utility room, as in some flats, you can still sometimes find some space outside the kitchen. For example, washing machines can go in a bathroom, ironing boards can be kept in a spare bedroom or even tucked into the corner of a landing, and vacuum cleaners are more convenient in a cupboard in the most-often-cleaned carpeted room.

As for storage for your bulk stores, if you have only limited storage space you will just have to comfort yourself with the thought that you are saving money by only paying for a small amount of living space rather than by getting the maximum discounts on stores bought in bulk!

Utility rooms like these which are a pleasure to work in — and even do the ironing in — also earn their keep by removing clutter from the kitchen and storing it all unobtrusively. This range of units incorporates some of the most useful new storage ideas to make life easier.

Right above. Plenty of space is an essential ingredient for a well-ordered laundry room. Here the washing machine and tumble dryer stacked one above the other free more floor space. You can wheel in bulky equipment — like the rotary iron here. Or have space for other activities, such as large-scale sewing projects — cutting out floor-length curtains, for instance. Note the bank of units above which can provide clean, safe storage for trolleyloads of stores and cleaning materials.

Right below. A pull-out work top is invaluable in a small utility room where there isn't space for a permanent table, especially if, like this one, it is big enough to use as a sewing table and firm and stable enough to take the weight of your sewing machine.

Opposite. A pull-out laundry basket saves humping around the dirty clothes. This one is designed to be stored under the worktop and match the rest of the units. It is handily positioned here near the sink and the washing machine.

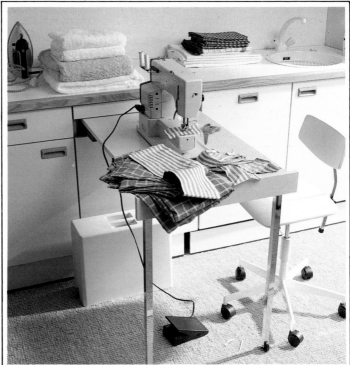